Return to Junction

SWAIM-PAUP SPORTS SERIES

Sponsored by James C. '74 & Debra Parchman Swaim
and T. Edgar '74 & Nancy Paup

Return to Junction

Smokey and the Bear and Other Aggie Football Stories

Gary Rollins '58

Foreword by

Jerry "Rat" Rhea '58

and

Ray "Grubworm" Stevens '58

Texas A&M University Press
College Station

First edition

This paper meets the requirements of ANSI/NISO Z39.48-1992 (Permanence of Paper).
Binding materials have been chosen for durability.
Manufactured in the United States of America

Library of Congress Cataloging-in-Publication Data

Names: Rollins, Gary, author. | Rhea, Jerry, writer of foreword. | Stevens, Ray R., writer of foreword.
Title: Return to Junction: Smokey and the Bear and other Aggie football stories / Gary Rollins '58; foreword by Jerry "Rat" Rhea '58 and Ray "Grubworm" Stevens '58.
Other titles: Swaim-Paup sports series.
Description: First edition. | College Station: Texas A&M University Press, [2020] | Series: Swaim-Paup sports series | Includes index.
Identifiers: LCCN 2019057941 | ISBN 9781623498658 (cloth) | ISBN 9781623498665 (ebook)
Subjects: LCSH: Bryant, Paul W. | Texas A&M Aggies (Football team)—History. | Texas A&M Aggies (Football team)—Biography. | Texas A&M University—Football. | Football coaches—United States—Biography. | Football—Texas—History.
Classification: LCC GV958.T44 R65 2020 | DDC 796.332/6309764242—dc23
LC record available at https://lccn.loc.gov/2019057941

Contents

A gallery of images follows page 80.

Foreword

What a wild and crazy ride it has been for the two of us. Sharing memories and telling and retelling tales that seem to get longer with the passing of each successive year.

We've known Gary for sixty-five years, and what he won't tell you is that he spent more than thirteen years at McCann-Erickson in four different offices and was, at varying times, the producer of Kern Tips's radio broadcasts of Southwest Conference football games. He handled the Texas Tourist Development Agency account as an account supervisor and later served as a speechwriter for Texas governor John Connally.

Gary managed both the radio and television networks for the Texas Rangers and the Houston Astros. The Astrodome was where he once reported for work. The next time you see a "Rainbow" Astros uniform, think of Gary. He quarterbacked that effort.

When the Southwest Conference was fading away, Gary was manager of corporate communications for Dr Pepper. Through his efforts, Dr Pepper is now the acknowledged lead supporter of football telecasts in both the Big 12 and the Southeastern Conference.

We first knew Gary as a student manager and, later, as sports editor of *The Battalion*. He skipped final exams in his senior year to recruit Jim Myers as athletic director and head football coach, replacing Coach Paul Bryant.

It worked. Myers was hired. Rollins and Jon Hagler, his companion in crime, were both allowed to take their final exams and move on with their lives. The next time you are on the campus, please make note of the Hagler Center, housing the Texas A&M Foundation, located just down the street from Kyle Field.

We join Gary in hoping you enjoy *Return to Junction*.

Jerry "Rat" Rhea '58 and Ray "Grubworm" Stevens '58

Preface

Howdy, Ags! Got a few stories for you.

Before you begin to embark on what I hope will be an enjoyable journey for you as we turn back the clock to that period of time in Aggieland that has come to be known as the Bryant era, here are some things you might want to know. The credit for this idea belongs to not one but two friends I first met when I became a student manager for Coach Paul Bryant's first three Texas A&M varsity teams. I later served throughout my senior year as sports editor of *The Battalion* at Texas A&M.

Jerry Rhea sprang the idea. He had accumulated a stack of personal letters sent to him by Charles "Smokey" Harper during the course of Rhea's outstanding career as an athletic trainer. These letters, all written on University of Alabama letterhead in a handsome cursive script, each contained a message that was both valuable and beautiful. Little did we know at that dim and distant time back in 1954, when it all began for us, that we would still be connected sixty-five years later through the Internet on an almost daily basis.

Jerry "Rat" Rhea was an outfit buddy of mine when we first arrived at Texas A&M. We first hooked up in "Dog" Battery, Field Artillery. Rat then embarked on a career-long path of achievement in the profession of athletic training. He served with considerable distinction in an athletic training career with the Los Angeles Rams and then, for more than twenty years, fulfilled the same role with the Atlanta Falcons. He ended his career after serving for many years for Rankin Smith, the team owner, who died in the 1990s, and Rankin's son, Taylor, the Falcons' president who followed in his father's footsteps.

Ray Stevens has roots in Mississippi and also served a similar term as a student trainer and, for a few years, achieved his goal of becoming a coach after leaving Texas A&M. He then expanded his knowledge base with additional advanced graduate degree studies. He's no stranger to academia. And he learned enough about athletic training to earn respect for the range and breadth of his knowledge.

Brothers Rhea and Stevens and I have shared the excitement and despair these past few years as we three experienced the agony and the ecstasy of watching Texas A&M play football on television. Every Saturday we were all dialed in, from Houston to Hattiesburg, Mississippi, to Atlanta, Georgia.

In truth, we had the benefit of living our lives as managers and trainers when Coach Bryant was calling the shots. We three knew and cherished the memories we shared about Smokey Harper, who was acknowledged to be Coach Bryant's most valued source of professional opinion. Over the years, it has saddened us to see the manner in which Smokey Harper has been depicted in both books and film. He registered a very strong and indelible impression.

The three of us have a once-in-a-lifetime opportunity to set the record straight about Smokey Harper. We have joined forces and, over the past six months, have made a thorough, conscientious effort to fill in all of the gaps about Smokey Harper—one last chance to set the record straight about a wonderful person. None of us had any awareness of the things Smokey had accomplished before setting foot on the A&M campus.

This expedition additionally gave us the opportunity to share the many stories, fables, tales, and memories we had each accumulated by virtue of the fact that we were there: every practice, every game day, and every year.

My role in sharing our findings with you has been supplemented and energized through the exhaustive efforts of Ray "Grubworm" Stevens. The guy can really dig up facts when you need them.

Please understand that the mission here is to share some wonderful times with those of you who follow the Texas Aggies and have been known to actually bleed maroon. Smokey was among the very first verifiable athletic trainers to come down the pike. He was an interesting, intelligent man, a superb athlete, a winning coach, a war hero, and a dear friend. He passed away a few years ago, but his memory will be etched in our minds forever.

We made every effort to check with each and every former teammate who might have a tale or two to share about things that happened with either Coach Bryant or Smokey Harper. We were there, and we were so very lucky to be right there at the beginning of the Bryant era. Most believe the

Bryant era is now long gone, although favorably remembered. Our feeling is that the Bryant era will continue to live as long as there are children and grandchildren who grew up loving Texas A&M.

Enjoy the book! Gig 'em!

Return to Junction

Chapter 1

Oldest Army

It was September 10, 1954—almost sixty-six years ago!—when thirty-five soon-to-be Texas Aggies arrived on the College Station campus and began to move in to Dorm 7 as members of "Dog" Battery, Field Artillery. Most arrived dragging foot lockers and apprehensively entered into a totally new life as members of the Class of '58. They were the fish of a class of 2,014, the largest first-year class in the school's history.

The incoming horde of freshmen cadets—the "fish"—were made aware of the fact that their standing on campus and on earth was lower than the lowest level of whale poop in the deepest ocean. Not even worthy of a capital F.

On that first move-in date, parents tearfully bade their sons good-bye, held hands and crossed their fingers, and headed back home, a scene that plays out each autumn to this very day. Back home to an empty bedroom with a Texas Aggies pennant on the wall. Back home to the dog who sadly sensed his best buddy was suddenly gone.

That year, 1954, was the first year the freshman class was integrated into the Corps of Cadets. Prior to that, from 1950 to 1953, they were freshman outfits housed separately at Bryan Air Force Base with a small cadre of upperclassmen to supervise them.

Upon our arrival on campus, there were only a small number of upperclassmen present. As the week moved along, the remainder of the upperclassmen troops rolled in. Snarling and snapping!

On this auspicious day, each new cadet in my unit had a slip of paper assigning him to "Dog" Battery, Field Artillery, a unit then residing in Dorm 7. Many still proudly wore their high school senior rings. By the end of the first day, the rings were history. And by the end of the second day, their schoolboy hair was gone, too.

Everyone also learned there was a possibility we would have "hair" privileges restored if and when the fish football team beat the University of Texas Shorthorns.

In November we did just that. We won hair privileges, thanks to John David Crow and a talented group of fish teammates, when we pasted the 'sips 20-7.

To clarify: fish cadets were "skinheads." Having hair privileges meant a buzz-cut military hairdo.

I can still recall one young fellow who, after checking out the mayhem in Dorm 7, decided Texas A&M was not the place for him, so he and his parents trekked back to their car with his footlocker in tow. He had lasted less than an hour.

In short order, uniforms were issued and rules for maintenance of each fish room in Dorm 7 were mandated. There were many indoctrination sessions focusing on the basics.

By the end of the first week, the fish class of Dog Battery had already downsized by eight souls to twenty-seven. Homesickness took a toll. Separation from that girlfriend back home doomed a few others. Some bolted after realizing the professors and instructors were no-nonsense people with not that much leniency for underperformers in class.

After the first six weeks, a sizable number of guys left, realizing they simply could not handle the scholastic requirements. Another handful of guys staggered around as they tried to decipher the "Dear John" letter that suddenly popped up in their new mailbox at the Memorial Student Center —the MSC.

But little did we know way, way back then that some of those fish buddies who entered our lives as we all entered manhood would actually still be with us, standing not quite as tall but quite proud, only sixty-six years later.

The new fish cadets were rudely introduced to a pack of wild-eyed, seemingly rabid sophomores who were intent on making the incoming fish lives miserable.

Prior to this year, upperclassmen would proudly own their personal paddles. They were individually designed with great care and creativity. Some had holes. But the paddles were for decoration purposes only. Anyone using the paddle was subject to immediate dismissal.

Typically, a fish might opt for four solid whacks with the straw end of a broom as "alternative punishment" to four hours on the Saturday Bull Ring.

Was there hazing? Absolutely. But the hazing was mostly emotional and not physical. Sitting in a "pink chair" or "hanging around the dorm" were substitute punishments. The former required a fish to stand with his back against the wall and then slide his rear end down until he neared a sitting position. Minus the chair, of course.

There were insulation-covered pipes in some rooms. The fish was ordered to hang from one of those pipes as long as he could.

Sophomores were "pissheads." Juniors were "serge butts," and the seniors were "leather legs." I strongly suspect the nomenclature remains approximately the same, with perhaps some differences now that young women are on campus and also in the Corps. What a big day it was when a young lady became cadet colonel of the Corps of Cadets.

We were quickly indoctrinated to clearly understand our new way of life. We came to anticipate the "Whistle Jock," who would loudly announce the arrival of a new day each morning at 6:00 a.m. We learned what was featured on the menu for that meal. And we learned the uniform of the day. We marched to chow three times each day. And those formations afforded the upperclassmen the opportunity to carefully peruse and abuse the demeanor and dress of each fish cadet.

Fish cadets were last in the pecking order at mealtime. Upperclassmen filled their plates first, in class order. And fish cadets were required to answer "cush" questions as a means of qualifying to enjoy dessert ("cush"). It was mandatory that you knew each food item on the table. "Bullneck" was meat. "Cow" was milk. "Sand and dirt" meant salt and pepper.

Each cadet quickly came to understand how important it was to "hit a brace" correctly. Here's a definition. The fish were required to place their back against a wall with the back of their heels, their fanny, and their shoulder blades and back of the head touching against the wall. That rigid position would force a fish to additionally pull his chin down onto his chest in order to form as many wrinkles in his chin as possible. The arms were positioned straight down against the side of the body. If and when a fish was told to hit a brace on the campus and there was no wall available, the fish would simply try to imagine there was a wall.

Pissheads never spoke in a normal tone of voice. They yelled. And they yelled up close in case a guy was hard of hearing.

"Whipping out" was a requirement that required substantial practice. Each cadet was required to memorize the name, home town, and major of each new upperclassman acquaintance. And woe befell the guy who failed to remember that fellow's pertinent details.

Every young cadet was ordered to speak to everyone with a loud "Howdy!" And if a cadet knew the other upperclassman, he would be expected to yell, "Howdy, Mr. Smith, Sir!"

Seniors were an impressive, albeit frightening group of guys. Very polished. Very worthy of respect. Scary almost.

One of our seniors in Dog Battery was a fellow from Tyler by the name of Jim Milstead. Not that many years later, his brother, Charlie Milstead, became one of Coach Paul Bryant's finer recruits in the Class of '60. He was an all-state quarterback with a golden arm and he unfortunately landed on a team that disdained passing. More to come on that topic.

There were a number of "orientation meetings" scheduled to give each of us an idea as to what was about to happen, and where, and when. Uniforms were issued. On-the-spot inspections were routine. Sitting in a hallway with knees tucked under our chins while being "indoctrinated" was an ongoing occurrence. Shoes needed to be polished—a lot!

We were provided with our class schedules and were immediately warned that the scholastic requirements were quite high and if a fish didn't clearly grasp that concept, he would probably be heading off campus after the first six weeks.

We learned about our unit's Six Point Study Plan. Translation: two feet in front of the four legs of the chair from 7:00 p.m. to 10:00 p.m. each evening. Officially, this was to be known as CQ—call to quarters.

Earlier, I referenced the subject of the paddles. Red ass—those were the words used to describe a guy's overall demeanor.

There was a lot of stress connected to living life as a fish: hazing, tough classes, and difficult professors. Instead of waltzing around with a smile on their faces, lots of guys simply said they were experiencing a case of the red ass. I imagine that can best be traced back to the days when the paddles were used. That would be when a red fanny would be the reason for a sour attitude immediately after a few whacks with the paddle.

Flunking an exam could give a fellow the red ass. Receiving a "Dear John" letter from the gal back home would definitely cause a chap to develop an even more intense case of the red ass. On the oft-traveled route between Houston and College Station, Highway 6, which was more of a road than a highway back then, there was a slight hill about ten miles south of the campus that I learned was known as "Red Ass Ridge." Why? Well, back then, which was when gasoline sold for twenty-five cents a gallon, the very thought of returning to the A&M campus after enjoying some time in Houston would typically give any Aggie the red ass.

The road we used to reach College Station was the same road to be followed on the way back home. If and when a fellow was pondering leaving Texas A&M, there was the reminder, "Highway 6 runs both ways." Putting it another way, if you don't like it, just leave.

As it happened, there were three fellows from Ennis High School who were assigned to Dog Battery. One was my fish old lady—my roommate—David Cox. The two others were Jerry "Rat" Rhea and Harry McBrierty.

A guy's "fish old lady" was his roommate and lifelong best pal. Those first couple of days, we had three guys in one small room, but the attrition reality quickly kicked in, and as the second week arrived, our third roomie was reassigned.

The "Boys from Ennis" are all still alive, retired, and enjoying Texas A&M football as a unit. Rat Rhea, who is a central part of the effort behind this book, became a student trainer and physical education major early in his junior year. We linked up during his junior year at Kyle Field. I was the senior student manager that year. Rat and I still talk weekly—sometimes daily—sixty-six years later.

Each fish required permission from an upperclassman to visit the "crapper," and special attire was required on those occasions. Vaguely I remember that fish were required to wear "piss pots and ponchos"—that is, helmet liners and rain ponchos—each time we found it necessary to visit the crapper. When the shower was in use, each cadet was expected to yell "Crapper!" before flushing the john. Flushing would typically cause hot water in the shower to suddenly turn icy cold. The shout was considered a courtesy gesture.

All fish learned quickly that information was largely shared through dissemination of a "crapper rumor." Sometimes crapper rumors were "good bull"—valuable information.

In my very first formation one warm September morning, the commanding officer of Dog Battery, Mr. Ed Forshage, a civil engineering major from Seguin, eased up very close to my face and asked, "When did you last shave, fish Rollins?"

The answer to that question was "Never, sir!"

He ordered me to return to my "hole"—my dorm room—immediately and shave. Forthwith.

I had neither a razor nor shaving cream, so I used fish Cox's stash and hurried back to formation. From that point I shaved every day—with my new razor!—every day, whether I needed it or not.

Perhaps one of the most memorable events of that first few weeks on campus was our very first Yell Practice in the Grove.

Historically, this was not Coach Bryant's first Yell Practice at Texas A&M. That memorable event occurred but a short time after he arrived on campus and will be reviewed in detail later in this book.

Our unit marched to that event with all of the pissheads in full voice. I had never heard so much yelling. The yell leaders tested our knowledge of the new yells and then, in a scene that is welded into our collective memories, Coach Paul "Bear" Bryant took the stage. The assembled horde went wild! Coach Bryant removed his sport coat and tie, rolled up his sleeves, and threw his coat and tie on the stage. He then yelled, "Are y'all ready to win some football games?" The Grove damned near exploded!

Right then, we all knew something very special was about to begin. Coach Bryant whipped the Aggie crowd into a frenzy and promised to make each and every one of us excited about supporting our Texas A&M team. The first game was but two days later against Texas Tech on Kyle Field. We all yelled crazily and sang and rejoiced.

That particular night and that one momentous event was probably the most positive thing that had happened to each of us since arriving in Aggieland. Better yet, maybe it was the only positive thing that had happened.

On Saturday night, the Texas Tech Red Raiders rolled into town and absolutely thrashed the team of "Junction Boys" who had worked so hard and seen so many of their teammates fall by the wayside. The Red Raiders were bigger, faster, and more talented. The final score of 41-9 was not that close. That was the first time we were all reminded that the Texas Aggies never lose a game. We may be outscored from time to time, but the most plausible reason is that we simply ran out of time.

During the 1957 season, that defeat was avenged when Texas A&M pounded the Red Raiders from the very first play. As the game ended, the scoreboard read:

Texas A&M 40
Texas Tech 7

When the Class of '58 gathered together to celebrate their fiftieth reunion, some discussion ensued when those of us tried to remember if our esteemed class exceeded the parameters to be called "Old Army." It was universally agreed that the Class of '58 was worthy of being forevermore known as Oldest Army!

Interesting sidenote: inasmuch as this was a Field Artillery unit, when the fiftieth reunion of Dog Battery was staged, virtually every guy wore hearing aids.

And no, hang on as we review the magnificent, memorable things that happened for all of us as we enjoyed being a part of the Bryant era at Texas A&M.

Chapter 2

When Did the Bryant Era Really Begin?

That's a challenging question. It brings to mind a quote I have long remembered that says, "I can explain it to you, but I cannot understand it for you." I've pieced together some of the relevant issues and tried to allow plenty of latitude at both ends of the era.

It appears highly probable that Coach Paul Bryant first began to experience a case of "happy feet" during the 1953 football season, when he was in his eighth season as head football coach for the University of Kentucky Wildcats. He coached the Wildcats for eight seasons. Their first bowl appearance was in 1947, and his 1950 team won its first Southeastern Conference title in 1950. That team finished the season 11-1 and with a victory over Bud Wilkinson's No. 1–ranked Oklahoma Sooners in the Sugar Bowl.

Bryant also led the Kentucky Wildcats to appearances in the Great Lakes Bowl, Orange Bowl, and Cotton Bowl Classic. In short, he had done one helluva job as head coach of the Kentucky Wildcats.

Bryant ultimately resigned at the end of the 1953 season because he felt Adolph Rupp's basketball team would always be the school's primary sports focus. There simply wasn't enough oxygen in the room for two hugely talented coaches to coexist. Kentucky was then what it is today—a basketball college.

It is relevant to point out the two later resumed their friendship and professionally assisted each other from time to time. But during that same final season, Bryant's home state of Arkansas set the wheels in motion to move Coach Bryant back to his home state. Bryant grew up in Moro Bottom, Arkansas.

With his record, Bryant realized other schools would soon come knocking, and he wanted to do what was best for his family and his career. When Texas A&M came calling, he was both interested and prepared. Texas A&M offered, and Coach Bryant accepted.

Thus, the clock began ticking on the Bryant era on January 1, 1954, as he began planning for the family to move to College Station. Coach Ray Graves was the preceding head football coach at Texas A&M and although his team fought long and hard, the competition was simply too stiff for the kind of success Texas A&M fans wanted for their football program.

It is relevant to point out one of the key pieces of the emerging puzzle was Willie Zapalac, who was a holdover coach from Graves's staff. Zapalac was a popular, well-connected assistant coach who had successfully approached and recruited Jack Pardee, a tall, athletic kid from Christoval, out in West Texas. That tiny community was so small that they played six-man football. Pardee, therefore, was already a "both ways" player and, inasmuch as the college game had morphed in 1953 to "both ways" football, having a fellow who was big, fast, and athletic—and had played both ways—was a huge plus. Simply stated, each player was required to master not one but two positions: one on offense and the other on defense.

When Coach Bryant first met and assessed the players put on the roster by a departing Coach Graves, there were three players who were destined to ultimately earn his respect at the preseason training camp in Junction prior to the start of the 1954 season. Jack Pardee, Dennis Goehring, and Gene Stallings were the linchpins for that group of young players, but a few others, including Billy Pete Huddleston, Marvin Tate, Herb Wolf, Fred Broussard, and Lloyd Hale, also played major leadership roles.

Pardee and Stallings both eventually became highly successful college and NFL coaches. Many of the players in the squad went on to accomplish things that border on the unbelievable. One of them won a PGA championship. Another rose to become the world's foremost orthopedic surgeon, specializing in knee reconstruction.

At that time this all began, none of us could have known that we were a part of an era in collegiate sports unlike any other in the history of college football. And although many of the key players and coaches and others directly involved in the activities of this special time are now both long departed and fondly remembered, we have made every effort to accurately retrace the footsteps and tell the accumulated stories the best we can.

It was both an exciting venture and a challenge. Asking a fellow what he remembers from a play or a drive in a game that took place in the third quarter of, say, the 1957 A&M–Texas game is way north of a "challenge." Some of these delightful old fellows cannot recall what they did yesterday! But, to a man, they remember being a part of the Bryant era.

One final point: All of us, to a man, realized it was never, ever a good idea to refer to Coach Paul Bryant as "Bear." He preferred "Coach Bryant." If and when anyone chose to call this great man "Bear," we immediately knew he was talking through his hat. His assistant coaches called him "Coach." His players called him "Coach." For all I know, his wife, Mary Harmon Bryant, called him "Coach."

There were some exceptions to this rule, however. A few coaching friends—all lifelong pals—had obviously earned the professional privilege of calling him "Bear." I guess that would be the equivalent of "dropping handles" with a fellow classmate. If Henry "Red" Sanders called Coach Bryant anything other than "Bear," it just wouldn't seem right.

One Aggie pal reminded me that fellow classmates enjoy calling each other with names that date back to the mid-50s. Rat Rhea and Grubworm Stevens, who have collaborated with me on this book, fall into that category.

This book was fun to both research and write. How honored we all felt to review the files and records in order to accurately share some interesting, compelling stories. Being a part of the Bryant era was an honor. We just did not know it at the time.

Enjoy yourself as we drag you back to an interesting time in Aggieland, beginning on January 1, 1954. When will the Bryant era end? Another intriguing question. The best answer, I believe, is that it will continue as long as there are children and grandchildren and even great-grandchildren who listen raptly as the family stories from the Bryant era at Texas A&M are told—and retold. What a special treat it is to retell the stories from a very special time in the history of Texas A&M football. Tighten your cleats and buckle your chinstraps!

Chapter 3

Howdy, Rat and Grubworm!

At some point during my three years at San Jacinto High School in Houston, I found myself leaning toward Texas A&M as the college I wanted to attend if and when I finally graduated. I had buddies a year or two older who preceded me as they ventured into the Brazos Valley, and they encouraged me to give Texas A&M serious consideration.

Why, you say? Maybe it was those darned ROTC uniforms. It certainly wasn't the girls!

Our family was far from affluent, but like many kids in my high school, I worked hard to build a nest egg to help me through at least my first year. I worked at numerous part-time jobs because family funds were severely limited. I was a decent teen baseball player and valued the support and encouragement of Lee Roy "Duck" Ashmore, my summer league baseball coach. He was a St. Louis Cardinals scout and arranged for me to pitch batting practice for the Houston Buffs on a couple of occasions. He had a good relationship with Roy Chester "Beau" Bell, the Aggies' varsity baseball coach, and was successful in his efforts to generate an offer of a spring sports scholarship to Texas A&M to play baseball.

Granted, this was a long time ago. A "spring sports grant-in-aid scholarship" was sufficient to assure payment for classes and books and housing while at Texas A&M for the spring semester. Nevertheless, it was a thrilling moment when I received the good news.

However, in the middle of the spring of my senior year, I—along with all other kids who received spring sports scholarships from Texas A&M—received a letter from Coach Bryant, the new athletic director—apprising me that all spring sports scholarships had been canceled. I was devastated!

As I sought to regroup, I learned I had been accepted by Texas A&M for the fall semester. Coach Ashmore and I met at Buff Stadium, out on the then-new Southwest Freeway, and he suggested I might want to take advantage of an opportunity to play baseball in Kansas in what would be considered a forerunner of Rookie League baseball. I leapt at the chance and rented a bedroom with some fine folks outside Kansas City and played in two or sometimes three games a week. I filled in the blanks working for the AT&SF Railroad in the Argentine Yards. It wasn't that much money. Almost a minimum hourly wage, but it was a beginning for me.

I earned almost enough money to make it through the second half of the school year, but found myself enrolled at Texas A&M and residing in Dorm 7 when I received word from the Athletic Department that I was invited to meet Coach Bryant in his office at Kyle Field. He was a huge, almost foreboding presence and, after welcoming me, assured me my scholarship offer was reinstated and I would now be welcomed as a member of the A&M baseball squad.

I was stunned. I told him I had forfeited my ability to play college baseball and immediately reflected back on the thought that I might have made a huge mistake.

Coach Bryant was quick to respond. He apologized for canceling my scholarship and then offered me a job on the football team as either a student manager or a student trainer.

I opted for the former, inasmuch as I knew squat about being an athletic trainer, so I was told to report to Smokey Harper, who was quite busy preparing for the varsity trip to Junction for preseason training.

Smokey introduced me to Troy Summerlin, the sophomore student manager, and my duties as an on-field manager were spelled out. Summerlin was preparing for the trip to Junction, but I was available to help the mostly student coaching staff with the early fish team workouts. Summerlin and I were both field managers. There were other student managers assigned to equipment and locker room tasks.

It was a chaotic beginning. All told, I recall there were probably about fifty or sixty young first-year athletes anxious to play football at Texas A&M. Workouts were scheduled both in the morning hours when it was cool and in the late afternoon. The squad had a large number of highly regarded football players. And there were a whole bunch who were not that athletically talented.

Rosters were posted each day reflecting both the daily position rankings and team assignments along with what part of the practice field was initially assigned for daily workouts. One important element each week was the posting of player weights.

All of the players wore white jerseys, gray pants, and white helmets. Colored slipover vests were used to denote which team was assigned for each player. Maroon jerseys were first-teamers. As I can best recall, blue jerseys were second team, green third, and so on. If a guy was on the yellow Scout Team, it was pretty easy to conclude the climb ahead would be both difficult and physically demanding. On the other hand, some guys were eager to compete as "walk-ons" because that was less stressful than being subjected to a bunch of demanding upperclassmen in their Corps of Cadets outfits. Also, there was always the possibility that someone without a scholarship might be offered one as a result of his performance at practices.

Although I was focused on learning my new on-field assignments, I feel pretty sure it was at that point I first met Grubworm Stevens. Grubworm grew up in Mississippi and was a fish cadet in Company A, Signal Corps. Rat Rhea, my Dog Battery buddy, joined the training staff at the beginning of the second semester of his junior year.

We were all kept quite busy. But as the days became weeks and then years, we three became lifelong friends.

The records will reflect that the varsity team spent a total of ten days in Junction. This was, of course, the birthplace for what would become the Junction Boys legend. On the eighth day, in the midst of a hard, hot, dusty scrimmage, the Aggies' All–Southwest Conference center, a big fellow by the name of Fred Broussard, suddenly decided to leave the on-field scrimmage and retreat to the sideline to regain his composure. He had been on the receiving end of harsh criticism from the coaching staff and from Coach Bryant.

When he cooled down, he returned to the huddle and offered his apology and asked permission to return to the practice. Coach Bryant denied his request and told him to pack his gear and take the bus back to Aggieland. Broussard had reached a point where he felt he could not take it, so he departed. Coach Bryant then looked around and asked if there was anyone present who had played center in high school.

Only one fellow raised his hand. It was none other than Troy Summerlin, the sophomore student manager. Troy weighed only 152 pounds. But that didn't manner. He could snap the ball. So Bryant sent him to the locker room to suit up, and at that moment he morphed from student manager to varsity. A very small center.

A call was placed back to the dressing room on Kyle Field, and I learned I was needed in Junction to fill in the gap created by Summerlin's on-field promotion. I hadn't even attended my first class and I was suddenly the sophomore student manager. It was something like a "battlefield promotion."

I was handed keys to one of the Athletic Department's white State of Texas sedans and loaded a box of training/practice supplies that were requested from Junction. As I rolled out, I stopped at a nearby Humble (now Exxon) gas station and picked up a map that would show me how to drive to Junction. It was about a four-hour drive and I managed to land in Junction right after chow that evening.

My chores included spending time with Summerlin—between practices—to learn what I would be expected to do when drills commenced behind Kyle Field. God, it was hot! And dusty.

Most of my time in Junction was spent preparing to come back to College Station. Packing gear and trying so very hard to stay out of the way. Smokey was both helpful and encouraging. Troy filled in the blanks for me as I stumbled along.

It never occurred to me that I had failed to notify anyone in Dog Battery that I was summoned to Junction. Those who missed me simply thought I had left campus and returned to Houston.

I left Junction one day before the single bus returned to College Station. I had the sedan packed with gear and managed to offload it at Kyle Field before reporting back to my outfit. As I can best recall, I went straight to Homer Martin, our first sergeant, and explained where I had been and why.

I escaped punishment from the ranking junior cadet, but I was sternly warned that it was truly a stupid move on my part to leave without telling anyone. I had already figured that one out. My mission, therefore, was to resume my cadet life as rapidly as possible. I was still a poor, dumb fish in every way and realized there were upperclassmen who were not at all pleased with my "excused absences" from formations and drills.

I was still euphoric, realizing I had been provided with the security of knowing I could attend my first full year without sweating the finances on a daily basis. There was the matter of academics, of course, and I recall it was about mid-semester that the Accounting 101 professor suggested I might find some other major less challenging than accounting. And so as quickly and expeditiously as I could, I jumped from accounting to journalism. It comforted me to later learn most guys changed majors at least once.

I now flash back to an event that occurred when Joe Namath was a quarterback at Alabama. His Bryant-coached team won the national championships and Namath was a talented, athletic kid from Pennsylvania. Namath had to work very hard in his classes to stay eligible. One day a New York writer tried to jangle Broadway Joe by asking if he majored in "basket weaving." Namath said, "Nah, man. I majored in journalism. It was easier."

The rest, of course, is history that is still being rewritten.

Chapter 4

It Ain't Always What You Know . . .

As the ideas for this book were coming into sharper focus, I thought that learning more about Jerry Rhea's pathway to a life in which he earned an outstanding reputation as an athletic trainer would be an interesting story. Although we were suddenly aligned as support-level guys—managers and trainers—for the Texas Aggies football teams, both fish and varsity—I never really knew how Rat approached the idea of becoming an athletic trainer.

Here is his story, as told in first person.

Reflections on Smokey Harper

How did I go from Dorm 13 on the second stoop to Smokey Harper? Great question! I came to Texas A&M from Ennis, a pleasant rural community about thirty miles south of Dallas. At Texas A&M I found myself in the company of three high school buddies, David Cox, Harry McBrierty, and Robert Stolusky. We were all assigned to Dog Battery, where I first also met Gary Rollins, Cox's fish old lady (that's Corps-speak for "roomie").

I had made good grades in Ennis and excelled in math courses, so I felt I was on a good track for majoring in engineering. An electrical engineering degree would also mean I would be making good money!

Somewhere along the way, as I learned also happened to almost every '58-er classmate, reality kicked in: I changed majors. I was a first-semester sophomore when I reached a mutual understanding with the people who ran the EE program that my plans for becoming a well-paid electrical engineer were not going to happen. Suddenly, I was faced with the challenge of selecting another route to fame and fortune.

What was I good at? I really didn't know the answer to that one. What would I like to do? Ditto.

I had always loved sports, but I wasn't really good at sports. I played football in high school but seldom played in a game. I loved being around my buddies who were good at sports, but I was lacking the tools to make me a success in either football or basketball. I ended up as the manager for the Ennis Lions basketball team and really enjoyed the thrill and excitement of being a part of a team.

I had read a book about Doak Walker and his time at Southern Methodist University, and it mentioned a man named Wayne Rudy, the SMU trainer. I learned about his job and some of the things he did for the SMU Mustangs. I thought—just maybe?—that was something I could do and might actually like doing!

Fast-forward to mid-term in January 1956. How would I approach it? Robert Stolusky was also from Ennis and held a football scholarship to Texas A&M. I asked him who the A&M team trainer was and if he could help with an introduction.

That's when I first met Smokey. I told him I thought I would like to be an athletic trainer and asked if I could simply come in and observe what trainers actually do while they're on the job.

He said, "Boy, you should stick with engineering because you'll make a lot more money that way." He then—reluctantly—agreed to let me be an observer during spring practice.

I changed my major to physical education, the only degree that would teach me anatomy, physiology, kinesiology, and other basic sciences. I next began reporting to the training room each afternoon after classes and hanging out there until dinnertime. Frequently, I didn't leave until after dinnertime.

Then spring training began. I was hooked.

An interesting sidenote next comes into focus for me. It was the first day of spring training and I was in the training room as Smokey, Billy Pickard, Ray Stevens, and Carl Merrell were prepping the team with tapes and bandages. I was really in the way, and I recall it was Billy who suggested I just go on out to the practice field and wait until practice started.

Practice that first day was on Kyle Field, which was unusual, because practices typically took place behind the west side of Kyle Field. So there I was, marveling: here I am! I was on the north end of Kyle Field and standing between the track and stadium seats—all by myself—when suddenly I was aware that someone else had just joined me on Kyle Field at the 50-yard line and was singing, in a very low bass, "Jesus Loves Me."

Good lord! It was Coach Paul Bryant, and I thought, "Here is this big, rough, tough, nationally acclaimed head football coach who worked the entire Corps of Cadets into a frenzy at that very first Yell Practice I attended in September 1954. He's singing 'Jesus Loves Me.'"

I later learned from Gene Stallings, then a player and later a very famous coach in his own right, that when Coach Bryant was singing "Jesus Loves Me," a very difficult practice was on the near horizon.

Getting My Feet Wet

That spring, Smokey very patiently taught me a few of the basics, but in truth I learned more from watching his three student trainers. I was relegated to chores that included cleaning the whirlpools, sweeping the area, and rolling ankle wraps and Ace bandages.

Smokey taught me how to tape ankles and sent me home that summer with a case of adhesive athletic tape and a book called the *Cramer Manual*, which had basic athletic trainer guidelines and illustrations for taping and bandaging hands, knees, and shoulders—the basics of athletic training. That summer, I availed myself of the opportunity to practice my newly acquired taping skills at night. My patient, long-enduring subject, Beverly, soon became my wife. She patiently endured the discomfort as I practiced. She also overlooked my bad techniques each night and—even worse!—the torment of having to pull the tape off her tender ankles.

That practice paid off. When I returned to the campus in September, I proved my newfound capabilities and earned a slot on the taping bench, where I continued to improve my taping techniques. In addition to the practice routines, I was commissioned to participate in the pregame activities both in the training room and on the field. I even traveled to some of the away games.

Smokey patiently taught me valuable lessons each and every day without ever saying, "This is how you do it." I learned so very much by simply watching Smokey and my fellow student trainers. It was fascinating! I marveled at their taping skills and their massage techniques and their use of modalities. More than anything else, I admired the way they communicated with the athletes.

Through my final two and a half years of my time at Texas A&M, I assumed more and more responsibility and developed a deep-seated love and respect for the profession that ultimately provided me with thirty-five years of fantastic memories and enjoyable experiences. I have to credit Smokey for that beginning. He was so genuine. He cared deeply for his job and for the young men he was molding to follow in his footsteps. I learned to love that man. And although he passed away many years ago, I love the memories to this very day.

Here's what was revealed to me about Smokey on a day-by-day basis. I was born in Texas and raised in Texas. We ventured into Oklahoma only a few times to visit relatives. Thus, when I entered Texas A&M in the autumn of 1954, Smokey Harper was the first real Southern gentleman I had ever met. I came to love his Southern accent and the phrasing he used that he formed during all of those growing-up years in Georgia, Tennessee, Kentucky, and Alabama. He had a truly infectious laugh.

He could be considerate and tender. He could also go after you with harsh words when that was a deserved response.

Smokey was an extremely loyal person, in particular to Coach Bryant, but he also defended his coaches and all their programs and requirements. Above all, Smokey cared about "his boys": the young athletes under his care. He treated both their bodies and their minds. I loved to hear him talk to the athletes casually, as he was taping or treating them for practice. Sometimes he would encourage them; other times he would scold them for not giving their best effort.

Smokey talked to "his boys" about alcohol and drinking responsibility. In the fifties it was illegal to drink if one was under twenty-one years of age. He knew legal or illegal did not make a difference to most college-age boys. He referred to liquor as John Barleycorn. "You can fight ol' John a lot of rounds," he would say, "but John Barleycorn will get you in the end—every time!"

When you get right down to it, Smokey Harper was a pioneer for the profession that was destined to become athletic training. He made it into a profession. Before Smokey came along, we were all just trainers.

When Smokey was in school, there were few courses that would prepare young men (and later, women) to assume the responsibilities for caring for athletes. Having been an athlete himself, he knew the other side of being injured. At that time there were few books available that broached this subject. You couldn't educate yourself with books.

Smokey took his job seriously. He cared about his players and wanted to keep them on the field. Yet Smokey had a great sense of humor. He would join in on practical jokes with his players and laugh and cut up with them. His players loved him.

I always considered Smokey to be a sneaky teacher. By that I mean he taught me things when I wasn't paying that much attention. He just had an ability to effectively teach a lesson and you wouldn't realize what he had done until many days later. Talk about a skill!

One of my favorite teaching points came one night at a home game on Kyle Field. We were all dressed in white pants, white shirts, white caps, white shoes, and socks. We looked like a battalion from the Mr. Clean Army. On game day we all dressed alike: so pretty and proud and standing at the ready on the sideline.

On this particular night, we had a player suddenly go down at about the 20-yard line near the hash mark at the north end of Kyle Field. The fellow was thrashing about in obvious pain, his arms moving wildly. I ran out onto the field as fast as I could and realized Smokey wasn't with me. I then looked back over my shoulder and saw him following me at a much slower pace. I must have flashed him a look that said, 'Why aren't you moving faster?"

He noted that look and spotted my frown and simply said, "Boy, when they *don't* move, you *hurry*!"

Over the many years, I read a lot about emergency care. I have attended an endless list of professional meetings and seminars, but I never heard a simpler, more inclusive lecture than the one Smokey taught me about the "emergency" part of emergency care. I have shared this very same story with many other trainers over my lifetime in the profession because it is so very practical.

In the spring of 1958, with graduation approaching, I knew I was going into the US Army for six months of active duty training. Then, in the spring of 1959, I would be looking for a job as a trainer. In Texas, even way back then, many high schools had full-time athletic trainers. The abundance of oil enriched the Texas Gulf Coast and West Texas, along with the budgets of high school sports programs. Many sizable communities had money available to hire good people, and they truly paid well.

Late in 1958 I heard that out there in West Texas—in Odessa—there would be a new high school opening in the fall of 1959 and they would be hiring an athletic trainer. The athletic director in Odessa was a Texas Aggie by the name of Cooper Robbins. He had twin sons, Ronald and Donald, who both played football at A&M. Of course, I knew both of these fine young men. I called Robbins and asked for an interview. He encouraged me to come to Odessa and I spent a day with him.

A few weeks later, Robbins offered me the job by phone, starting in August of 1959. He included a salary quotation. I immediately went to Smokey and asked him what he thought about the offer. What should I do?

When he heard the salary they were prepared to pay, he said, "Boy, if you don't take it, I will!" I took the job and worked in Odessa for the next eight years. Smokey had given me an excellent recommendation that helped start my professional career.

So this was just the first of many occasions when I realized the importance and value of a strong alliance with both Smokey Harper and those closely tied to the Bryant era at Texas A&M. And I have more I want to share!

Smokey Harper: A True Friend

As my career moved along from high school to a position with the Los Angeles Rams—one of my life goals—my relationship with Smokey Harper continued to grow.

When Coach Bryant responded to a siren call from Alabama, his "Mama," Smokey stayed behind and served Coach Jim Myers in the same capacity as before. His tenure as a State of Texas employee was of value to him and, as I can vaguely recall, Coach Jim Myers once stepped forward when an effort was made to remove and replace Smokey; he reminded those above him that Smokey was close to retiring, and firing him might jeopardize his tenure.

Smokey Harper remained at Texas A&M until he was eligible to retire. At that point, Coach Bryant offered him a job on his staff at Alabama, but instead of functioning as a full-time athletic trainer, he wanted Smokey to be available to the horde of supporters for social gatherings in nearby Tuscaloosa coffee shops. He became an ambassador for Coach Bryant, and everyone knew how much Coach Bryant admired and trusted Smokey. It was a dream job for Smokey.

Back in Texas, it made me proud that the Southwest Athletic Trainers Association (Texas and Arkansas) realized it was time to recognize Smokey Harper for his impressive achievements and his service as an athletic trainer.

Smokey never positioned himself as a "political" trainer. He was not active in either professional meetings or leadership. The members just thought it was high time to honor this fine, professional gentleman.

Coach Bryant, when he learned of this good news, was enthusiastically supportive and made immediate arrangements for Smokey to come to Waco to be honored by the SWATA membership. Smokey was warmly welcomed. He was thrilled, as well when he was elected to the National Athletic Trainers Association Hall of Fame.

It was back in my days in Odessa when Smokey and I first began corresponding. He became aware of my desire to move on up to a college setting, and he began to quietly advance my candidacy to a sizable number of players and coaches he had come to know personally over his long career. He had lots and lots of friends in the sports world. And so he began to call in favors from some of these men and making personal calls on my behalf. Not all of those calls ended in interviews, but all of them encouraged me to continue to keep on trying.

I interviewed with the Detroit Lions (Harry Gilmer, who played at Alabama when Smokey was in Tuscaloosa), the University of Kentucky (Charlie Bradshaw), and Northeast Louisiana (Dixie White). And during those years, Smokey was always trying to help me improve professionally. He would write to me each year in that marvelous, beautiful cursive handwriting, telling me about his new life at the University of Alabama. He kept checking on me to see if I was happy, satisfied, and eager for more challenges.

I enjoyed reading about Coach Bryant's task of trying to get the most out of those "undersized" players on the Bama roster. All of those letters were on University of Alabama letterhead, which also proclaimed yet another national championship won by those "undersized boys."

Smokey celebrated with me when I landed a job with the Los Angeles Rams and then again when I secured a position as head athletic trainer for the Atlanta Falcons. Smokey knew—deep down inside—that this was what I had always wanted.

When Smokey died in the summer of 1970, I was in training camp with the Falcons at East Tennessee State in Johnson City, Tennessee, and was unable to attend his funeral.

Now, sixty years after leaving Texas A&M, I still treasure my time with him as a mentor, a friend, and the first true Southern gentleman I personally came to know. I dearly loved that man.

Chapter 5

You Can Call Me Grubworm

I first met Ray Stevens, a smiling, blond guy from Jackson, Mississippi, that first week of football practice in September 1954 at Kyle Field. I was brand new as a student manager, and he had just finished mustering-in with Smokey Harper in the training room.

We introduced ourselves as fish Rollins and fish Stevens and immediately dropped handles and became known to each other as Gary and Grubworm!

One evening while dining at the training table, it was none other than Jack Pardee who first called fish Stevens Grubworm. What a great name!

I later learned that Grubworm had spent most of his life in Jackson, but he had been born in Houston and had many relatives living in North Texas. He knew about Texas A&M, but not that much. He also espoused an interest in SMU when the time came to zero in on a college. I guess it was the allure of Doak Walker that registered a favorable impression. But SMU was way too expensive. Texas A&M was a bargain, comparatively speaking.

As we exchanged stories about how each of us managed to be where we were, I chuckled as I learned he had first been sent to interview with a fellow called Billy Prichard. His "downfield blocker" in that effort was a man he had met at Junction when he attended a six-week summer session for new students. Texas A&M had sent a letter to Grubworm's father suggesting he take that a six-week course as a means of preparing for college-level courses. The site was Junction, and the memories of his time in that place stay with him to this very day.

By attending this course, a new freshman student had the opportunity to arrive on campus with credit for seven hours of course work: English 101, a beginning math course, and a smaller credit for physical education. And taught by real instructors, not upperclassmen TAs.

It was at Junction that he first met Les Palmer, who was assistant baseball coach and physical education professor back in Aggieland. They struck up a conversation that evolved into a friendship.

Grubworm came to Texas A&M because he had aspirations of becoming a football coach. The way he explained it, he wasn't smart enough for an academic scholarship and not talented enough, athletically speaking, for a jock scholarship. When he was attending Jackson's only high school, Central High School, he kept slipping down the depth chart on the football squad until he endorsed his move from football to track.

He wasn't particularly fast or that agile. But the track coach recommended he consider running the half-mile event. Once more, he fell short as a middle-distance runner and accepted a position as manager for the track team.

The track coach was also a football coach, and Grubworm was able to watch him tape ankles. For a brief spell, Grubworm had his ankles taped as well. One day he asked if he might have some instruction from the coach on ankle taping, and that opened the door to his developing interest in becoming an athletic trainer.

Grubworm is a sports nut and knew the full story about Coach Bryant coming to Texas A&M from Kentucky. He was delighted to have a chance to be a firsthand witness to a first-class college football program. What better place to learn how to be a coach than on Kyle Field!

He prevailed upon Les Palmer to suggest how he might be granted an interview to become a student trainer. Palmer recommended he go to Kyle Field and ask to see Bill Prichard, whom he described as "a guy who thinks he runs the place."

The very next day, he showed up in the training room when things were relatively quiet and asked to see Billy Prichard. Smokey Harper, who was standing nearby, said, "Billy, somebody is here to see you."

Grubworm suddenly found himself being addressed from very close range from a guy who bellowed, "My name is Billy Pickard. P-i-c-k-a-r-d! What do you want?"

Stevens stammered to both Billy and Smokey that he wanted to see if he could be considered for a position as student trainer. Smokey listened patiently and then told him to show up the next day when practice began.

He was hired. And he later realized Les Palmer had called and opened the door for him with Smokey.

Those first few days were spent following people around, watching the pre-practice taping, operating the whirlpool, and mainly staying out of the way. When the first game approached, he was wearing his whites and Pickard told him to "stay out of the way" on the sidelines and watch what was going on. Just in case he might actually learn something.

All things considered, it was a beginning. And he spent the next four years of his life learning from Smokey. Pickard was a junior and moved along to his first off-campus job. He later returned and spent the remainder of his career working various jobs in the Texas A&M Athletic Department after first working as head athletic trainer. He retired not that many years ago and, after his passing, was honored posthumously when the school named the Pickard Tunnel (under Wellborn Road) after him. The plaque spells his name correctly: Pickard, not Prichard.

As things were about to get underway at that first game, Pickard strolled back over and told Grubworm he needed to latch onto a towel and be prepared to dash out onto the field after the Fightin' Texas Aggie Band had played at halftime. He was instructed to watch Reveille closely, because Ms. Reveille would almost always race around the field, barking at the top of her doggie lungs. She would then pick a spot and poop. Grubworm's first official job as a student trainer was to quickly retrieve and secure the poop Reveille left behind. He even had a cup for the chore.

The four years he spent at Texas A&M were productive, memorable, and exciting. Like all of us, he came to regard Smokey Harper with great respect. Smokey taught guys how to do things the right way and then allowed them to learn and grow at their own pace.

Grub was joined in his third year by Rat Rhea, who had his sights firmly targeting a career as an athletic trainer. Both guys majored in physical education, which was the best place to be, whether a fellow wanted to be a coach or a trainer. Gene Stallings was a physical education major as well, but his exposure to Coach Paul Bryant as a mentor paid off for both of them in so many ways.

Grubworm graduated from Texas A&M and continued to advance his education in graduate school. He coached some, learned a lot, and spent many years in higher education. With Rat, he became a lifelong friend. Sixty-six years later, the three of us still agonize each weekend during football season. We all still bleed maroon.

Grubworm and his lovely wife, Joan, live in Hattiesburg and enjoy retired living in Mississippi, the state he grew to love when he was growing up. Rat finished a remarkable career after serving as head athletic trainer for both the Los Angeles Rams and the Atlanta Falcons. He maintained contact with Smokey Harper throughout his entire career as an athletic trainer. He should be credited for suggesting the need for a book that would be called *Return to Junction.*

It is touching to realize that a man with such an amazing record of accomplishments passed away in virtual obscurity. Sadly, there were books written about Texas A&M football and Junction and Coach Bryant that misrepresented Smokey Harper. He was caricatured in a film as a man who loved booze. And that was not the case at all. Smokey Harper was a one-of-a-kind hero of a man who enriched the lives of all those around him. Coach Bryant trusted him implicitly. And when he departed this tortured planet, he left a hole in each of our hearts.

Rest in peace, Smokey.

Chapter 6

Howdy! My Name Is Smokey

Working on this book has reminded me of something I learned about World War II in Europe, Gen. Dwight D. Eisenhower, and one of his obscure headquarters staff officers. Events about the war and General (later President) Eisenhower are well documented and generally known, but we know much less about the officers in Ike's command staff upon whom he greatly depended and whom he deeply admired. It seems unlikely that some scholarly historians could name even one of the Supreme Commander's team.

In the same manner, college football and its head football coaches have also been well chronicled since that first forward pass was thrown. But how many of their most ardent and faithful followers can name their favorite head football coach's staff? Probably not many.

Smokey Harper was an athletic trainer and an obscure but valued member of Coach Paul Bryant's staffs at the University of Kentucky and at Texas A&M. He so valued Smokey that, after Smokey retired from Texas A&M in 1961, Bryant hired him to take charge of the University of Alabama's football film operations. That was his job, but there were talented young people who could do the work. Instead, Coach Bryant wanted Smokey to be available as a good will ambassador: someone who could go out and have coffee with the local supporters if and when Coach Bryant was unavailable. Coach Bryant trusted Smokey's many skills and his unique ability to relate to people in a meaningful way. Smokey was Coach Bryant's Yoda, and he had great awareness of Smokey's ability to judge people—players, too.

In a nutshell, Smokey had two grades for any player whose capabilities were called into question. Smokey would tell Coach Bryant they were either "wuffashit" or they weren't.

Smokey learned about his role as athletic trainer at ground level. Simply put, athletic trainers are held responsible for taking care of the health of their athletes. They are the first responders, if you will, when a player is injured, and it follows that they are next involved in the treatment and rehabilitation of their athletes. The bulk of their work is done behind the scenes unless and until a player goes down on the field or the court.

Back then, there were but two or three cameras televising football games—as opposed to dozens of cameras now seen at every college game—and the trainer's role was never the focal point of the game. The athletic trainer's photo was sometimes included in the staff coaches grouping in the game programs. In a word, athletic trainers at that time were obscure.

Harper entered athletic training during the early years, beginning in 1927. His career included stops at the University of Alabama, Clemson, Florida, Kentucky, UCLA, Vanderbilt, and Texas A&M. He worked on the staffs of some of the nation's most famous coaches, including Josh Cody, Red Sanders, and Paul Bryant. He was the official trainer at most major bowl games of that era.

The first recognized athletic trainer in the United States was employed only seventeen years before Smokey was born. Until then, going all the way back to ancient Olympic games, a trainer was someone who prepared participants to compete in the Greek games.

In the spring of 1881, Harvard hired Great Britain's John Robertson to work with the school's track and field teams. He was experienced in training men in the fine art of running faster than their opponents. Harvard's hiring someone to carry out this job was an innovation in US college sports because traditionally students—upperclassmen—were in charge of directing their institutions' interscholastic athletic teams during the late 1800s and into the 1900s. The results of this innovation proved positive for the Harvard track and field team.

Later that same year, Harvard engineered another innovation that became the defining moment, one that would eventually affect the way management of athletic teams are organized and how the health of those teams' participants is guarded.

During the fall of 1881 the football team, seeking to attain the same level of success achieved with the track and field team, hired none other than John Robertson, again breaking with the prior custom of having students lead each college team.

Thus, the concept of today's athletic trainer was born. Harvard's idea immediately caught on, and other competing schools—Columbia, Princeton, Yale, and Michigan—all hired athletic trainers as well. The innovation spread quickly.

Those very early athletic trainers were all former athletes. Initially the main focus was on conditioning. Gradually, the focus widened, and attention shifted to recovering from injuries and applicable remedies. Injured athletes could be treated with an eye to getting them back on the playing field.

The blending of athletic training needs with medicine pushed the modern profession that would eventually be labeled "sports medicine." That descriptor finally arrived on the athletic scene a half century and two world wars later. The practice of medicine, at the very same time, was evolving to what it is today.

Smokey Harper was a pioneer in this newly emerging field of caring for the well-being of athletes under his protective umbrella. His life's work as one of the early athletic trainers was a precursor to today's medically recognized profession, accepted as an integral part of modern athletic programs.

Smokey Harper died in 1971. If he were peering over the reader's shoulder, he would interject surprise at being portrayed as a "pioneer" in the field of athletic training. If you asked him, he would probably reply, "I was just doing my job." And he would say it in a pleasant, infectious Georgia drawl that he never managed to lose.

All of us were struck by both his comments and his manner of speaking, which reflected a humble, unpretentious, and compassionate personality.

But before we get too far ahead, let's go back to the beginning. Mark the date: December 31, 1898. In a small farmhouse near Milledgeville, Georgia, a baby boy was born. The proud parents, John and Mamie Harper, named their baby boy Charles Edwin Harper.

Later the family would move to Macon, Georgia. Charles Harper was growing up in the early years of the 1900s, along with a new and popular sport—basketball. Baseball was already well established, with professional teams in most of the large eastern cities. Meanwhile, varsity football was being played at most college campuses across the land.

Charles was an enthusiastic, talented young athlete. He played both basketball and baseball in sandlot pickup games and on playgrounds with basketball goals. That sport was invented eight years before Charles was born, and the sport grew quickly through the YMCAs to high schools and then to the colleges.

Semiprofessional and minor league baseball teams were springing up like wildflowers in Georgia and, interestingly enough, Georgia quickly emerged as a hotbed for major league baseball talent. Between 1900 and 1919, over thirty Georgia lads made it to the major leagues, including the "Georgia Peach," Ty Cobb. Another was Doc Bass, who was from Macon. He was the same age as Charles, and they were teammates at Lanier High School.

We know Charles played baseball at Lanier High School because that is where he earned his handle, Smokey, a moniker that had nothing to do with his fastball.

Lanier had traveled to Milledgeville for a game. Charles, now a tenth grader, had made the team and was wearing his new uniform. Somewhere between Macon and Milledgeville the bus had stopped and—boys will be boys—some of the players, including Charles, bought cigars.

We can presume Charles must have been a pretty decent player inasmuch as this anecdote takes root in the visiting team's bullpen. Charles was his own man, and he lit up a cigar while hanging out in the bullpen. We know, too, that Charles was something of a ladies' man because his girlfriend had come to the game to see him play. She strolled over to the bullpen to chat with him while the game was underway and talked to him through the fence. So as to not offend his lady friend by smoking in front of her, he hurriedly stashed his lit stogie in his uniform's back pocket.

They chatted for a spell. And then the call came from the bench to put Charles in the game as a relief pitcher. Charles forgot all about the cigar as he warmed up.

Time to pitch! Charles sprinted from the bullpen to the pitcher's mound and threw his warm-up pitches. He checked the bleachers to see if he could locate his lady friend. The catcher makes the traditional toss to second base and the ball moves around the horn. As the third baseman hands Charles the ball, the seat of Charles' new baseball pants bursts into flames.

What happened thereafter is mostly unknown. What is known is that this was the moment everyone began calling Charles "Smokey," and the nickname caught fire, so to speak.

Smokey was an outstanding athlete on the Lanier High School basketball and baseball teams. He graduated in the spring of 1916. While he was learning algebra and studying American history, he nonetheless had to have been aware of the World War I battles being fought in Europe. Meanwhile, even though the United States had sought to remain neutral in the European conflict, troubles were also springing up in Mexico. It turns out that young Harper was aware of—and interested in—joining the battle. As required by his age, he sought his parents' permission to enlist, but they denied his request.

Not to be thwarted, Harper lied about his age and joined the Georgia National Guard on June 16, 1916, in defiance of his parents' wishes. He swapped his high school baseball uniform for military olive drab and khaki. Within weeks, he and his Georgia unit, the 2nd Georgia Infantry, were at the Macon train depot, preparing to move forward on their mission to proceed to the Rio Grande Valley in Texas to join in the hunt for the Mexican revolutionary Pancho Villa.

As he waved good-bye to his parents, he also waved good-bye to his teenage bearing. He was absolutely thrilled to embrace the life of a US Army private. He was about to get in on the action. He would soon join the fight to capture or even kill Pancho Villa, purported to be the murderer of so many fine, innocent Americans.

He had listened to the homefolk discussing the Texas-Mexican border troubles. Soon, he dreamed, they would be talking of his success when he returned home as a war hero. When he arrived at his post, he was assigned a tent and a cot and warned to check his shoes daily for scorpions. Also, he learned he should be on the lookout for rattlesnakes!

Private Harper quickly learned about army life. Instead of an armed search for Pancho Villa, he would spend most of his time pulling guard and KP duty while remaining vigilant for scorpions and rattlesnakes.

Fall turned into winter, and the spring of 1917 emerged. The tedious border guarding assignment ended, and Smokey's US Army life took a dramatic shift. The United States entered World War I in April 2017.

The Georgia National Guard, along with other state National Guard units, joined forces in the newly formed 42nd Infantry—later to become known as the Rainbow Division—at Camp Mills, Long Island, New York.

After outfitting and training, the 42nd would be one of the first US divisions to land in France. Smokey's Rainbow Division detachment was the 151st Machine Gun Battery, which was assigned to the 84th Infantry Brigade.

Once on French soil, they received more training. This round was on trench warfare. At the front and now in the trenches, the Rainbow Division participated in four major World War I operations: Champagne-Marne,

Aisne-Marne, the Battle of Saint-Mihiel, and Meuse-Argonne. The Battle of Saint-Mihiel included the 84th Infantry Brigade in the order of battle.

That bloody conflict was fought over a period of three days in September 1917. There were more than 4,000 American deaths and more than 7,000 wounded in battle. Machine gunners were, quite obviously, primary targets. Private Harper was caught in the crosshairs.

A shard of shrapnel hit him in his mouth, taking out a number of his teeth. A severely wounded Private Harper left the muddy, bloody trenches on a stretcher. After undergoing triage at the forward field medical aid station, he was sent to a hospital behind the lines.

The Rainbow Division made a triumphant voyage home after Armistice Day. On May 19, 1919, Private Smokey Harper returned to civilian life. He had joined the US Army and had a much more vivid experience than he could have imagined during his geography studies, just a few years earlier in high school.

During that part of his life, he lost many teeth and most of his hearing. Bear in mind that those of us who worked alongside Smokey Harper in the period 1954–58 were totally unaware of the fact that he was a combat veteran of World War I or that he had been seriously wounded. Those wounds caused his hearing loss, but never once did he mention the cause of it.

Texas A&M, with a long, strong military tradition, would have been so very proud to know that Charles "Smokey" Harper was both an outstanding war hero and a damned fine athletic trainer, whose mission was to teach those young fellows how to be good athletic trainers.

If we had only known then what we know now. But there is more. As we researched existing records, we realized we had lost track of Smokey when he suddenly left Mercer University at the halfway point in his senior year. Fortunately for him, his former coach knew exactly where to find him.

In the spring of 1927, Clemson University's new head football, basketball, and baseball coach hired Smokey Harper as a college athletic trainer. Coach Josh Cody hired an assistant coach in 1927—a Vanderbilt graduate like Cody—who, in his own right, would later become a successful head coach and also was significant in Smokey's career. The assistant was Henry "Red" Sanders. Cody, Sanders, and Smokey Harper would work together at Clemson for three more years.

In 1931 Coach Cody returned to Vanderbilt as an assistant football coach and basketball coach. Smokey was also hired at Vanderbilt as an athletic trainer, probably with Cody's recommendation. There he worked under head coach Dan McGugin until 1934, when McGugin retired as head coach and remained on board as athletic director. McGugin is the "winningest" football coach in Vanderbilt history.

When Cody gave up his head job at Clemson and returned to Vanderbilt, he knew McGugin was retiring in the near future. It was no secret that Cody wanted to be head coach of the Commodores, where he had been a star athlete. That was not to be, however. Ray Morrison replaced McGugin as head football coach. Morrison, a former Vanderbilt athlete, came to Vandy from SMU, where he had been head coach for twelve years and finished with 182 wins, 31 losses, and 20 ties.

Here's a little bit of trivia with an interesting connection to Smokey's future career. When Josh Cody left Clemson, he was replaced by Jess Neely, who would eventually become head coach at Rice and a fierce rival for Bryant. Matty Bell, who was head coach at Texas A&M from 1929 to 1933, replaced Morrison at SMU. Cody accepted the head coaching position at the University of Florida. Three years later, in 1938, when Morrison left Vanderbilt, Smokey went to the University of Florida. It was just a one-year interlude, because Cody moved to Temple University at the end of the next season. Smokey returned to Vanderbilt to serve under another Cody associate, an old friend from Clemson days and former Vanderbilt player, Red Sanders.

Head Coach Sanders needed a line coach. After scouting around, he hired a former player at the University of Alabama, who was then an assistant coach in Tuscaloosa. His name was Paul Bryant, and he was generally known by his nickname, "Bear." During the 1940 season, Coach Sanders developed appendicitis and assistant coach Bryant had to serve as the acting head football coach for one game. This marked the first time Smokey worked with Bryant as a head football coach, even though Bryant was actually acting head coach.

Within a few days of that game, Pearl Harbor was attacked, war was declared, and World War II was changing lives. Both Sanders and Bryant, like uncounted other coaches across the nation, would leave their jobs and join up for the duration. Smokey Harper was 4-F because of his hearing disability.

World War II required many, many adjustments and improvisations back home, including in college athletics. One such adjustment occurred in Nashville. The Commodores needed a basketball coach. Trainer Smokey Harper put on another hat and coached Vandy's 1943 basketball team. The results: 12 wins, 3 losses, for a .800 W-L percentage.

From the 1943 football season to 1946, Smokey worked as athletic trainer with Coach Frank Thomas at the University of Alabama, Paul Bryant's college coach. He made his move from Vanderbilt when Red Sanders joined the military. Thomas was his fifth head coach in seventeen years as a college trainer. Coach Thomas retired in 1946, Red Sanders returned to Vanderbilt, and Smokey was back in Nashville at his old job as Vanderbilt trainer for the third time. The next year, Sanders was hired as head coach of the UCLA Bruins, and he took Smokey out to Los Angeles.

But there was too much Southern blood coursing through Smokey's veins. He felt out of place in California. He heard about an athletic trainer job at the University of Kentucky. Smokey and the Bear would be on the same team, as had been the case in 1940 when assistant coach Bryant stepped up to replace his head coach.

When Smokey joined Coach Bryant in Lexington, he had already previously observed some of the most successful football coaches of the collegiate football coaching profession—Cody, McGugin, Thomas, and Sanders. He not only knew his trade as an athletic trainer but had also watched those head coaches handle their athletes; he had learned how to judge not only their physical talents but their psychological makeup as well.

Harper could draw upon his playing experience, his deadly combat trials in France, and, for twenty years, his daily observations of five coaches at the top of their profession. Coach Bryant recognized that it was one thing for a trainer to know how to handle an athlete's injuries and physical needs; to be able to address and appraise that athlete within the parameters of the requirements of a certain sport would have to be considered value added.

After eight seasons at the University of Kentucky—with 60 wins, 23 losses, and 6 ties; trips to the Orange, Sugar, and Cotton Bowls; and a national championship (although then "unofficial")—Coach Bryant was compelled to move on down the road at the end of the 1953 football season. It was the University of Kentucky's loss and the Agricultural and Mechanical College of Texas' gain.

We all met Smokey at the end of summer in 1954. He had come to the Brazos River bottom from the lush bluegrass of Kentucky earlier that year while we were all still in high school. At that time and for the next four years, as student trainers and student managers, we worked under his supervision. We were too young to grasp or even care about who Smokey really was and where he had been and what he had done. We were too wet behind the ears and preoccupied with our own lives to have any curiosity about this almost elderly person who dressed in the athletic trainer's uniform of that day: white pants, white shirt, white baseball cap. His graying hair, combed straight back, the emerging (perhaps premature) lines on his face, and his hearing aid were indications of the road he had traveled before we knew him. He had a remarkable, almost unbelievable story to tell, but unfortunately we never asked about his earlier life.

He just may have been one of the best teachers we ever knew. And we didn't know it at the time.

Chapter 7

When Wild Willie Met Gabby

Let the record show that Willie Zapalac was, first of all, a Texas Aggie. Zapalac was a Madisonville, Texas–born kid who grew up on a dairy farm in Bellville, where he rose each morning at 5:00 to take care of his family's chores before school. His mother would allow him to sleep late, until 6:00 a.m., on football game days. He was a five-sport letterman at Bellville High School and lettered four years in football, where he earned the name Wild Willie.

Why Wild Willie? Tighten your cleats. This is interesting. Wild Willie Zapalac led Bellville to an 11-0 season in 1938. Ten of those wins were shutouts. The 1938 squad was adjudged to be the best in Bellville's storied history. Against Caldwell, he rushed for 323 yards, which is still Bellville's only 300-yard rushing performance.

He was heavily recruited, of course, and ended up at Texas A&M in the fall of 1939, where he played on not just one but two Cotton Bowl teams. He was elected as Best Blocker for three consecutive years and served as the Aggies' captain in his senior year. He shared time on the field with his teammate, Jarrin' John Kimbrough, the Aggies' first Heisman Trophy candidate.

As World War II began, Zapalac volunteered for service and successfully completed thirty-two bombing missions as a navigator in the Seventh Air Force in the Pacific. He was next promoted to squadron bombardier for the 494th Bomber Squadron and ultimately retired from his military service with the rank of captain. Then it was back to football.

He was drafted by the Pittsburgh Steelers in 1947 and played for a short period of time, but injuries ultimately brought an end to his professional career and he then logged stops at McAllen and Hillsboro high schools before he next moved to a head coaching assignment at Arlington State College (now the University of Texas at Arlington).

Ray Graves, then the Texas A&M head football coach, considered Zapalac, because of his Texas A&M lineage, to be an important member of his coaching staff. Zapalac, it should be noted, was both well known and highly respected by virtually every coach in Texas. Many of those fellows had played against him in high school or college or both.

Zapalac was an excellent recruiter—one of the very best, along with Elmer Smith—but it takes no great leap of faith to realize there were probably more than a couple of West Texas coaches who suggested he take an up-close-and-personal look at a tall, gangly youngster in Christoval by the name of Jack Pardee.

Christoval is a tiny town not far from San Angelo. There were only enough students to field a six-man football team. Zapalac recruited all of Texas, but his hot zone was West Texas. At that time, places like Midland, Odessa, Lubbock, and San Antonio were known for being where high school football was the only show in town during the fall.

Bryant knew about Zapalac and retained him to be a member of his first coaching staff when he moved from Kentucky to Texas A&M. It is interesting to note that both Zapalac and Elmer Smith were encouraged to seek out "big, old country boys who weren't strangers to hard work and tough times." That description fit Jack Pardee to a T. Fact is, it also was the way Charlie Krueger was at first perceived when the Aggies zeroed in on him in the tiny town of Caldwell, which was not that far from the Texas A&M campus. That's another story covered in a later part of this book.

The Christoval coach facilitated a meet-up with Coach Zapalac and Pardee, and that initial chat was probably at a diner on the town square in Christoval. Christoval wasn't large enough to have a Dairy Queen. It's an even smaller community today.

It was something of a reach for Zapalac to even consider a kid who had only played six-man football, but there was definitely something different about Jack Pardee. He was a big kid. Very polite, because that's the way his parents raised him. And he found it hard to believe he would even be considered by Texas A&M. Furthermore, he was painfully quiet, an attribute that would eventually cause his teammates to give him the nickname "Gabby."

Zapalac sensed there might be other issues standing in the way: as the conversation continued, Pardee shared the news that his family could never afford to send him to a big-time college. He confessed his family couldn't begin to buy the clothes he would need. Even though that was an embarrassing disclosure, Zapalac sought to assure him that would be no problem at all. Texas A&M would provide clothing along with what would now be called a full ride—meaning a nice room, lots of good food, and a great study environment.

That did it. Pardee agreed. Zapalac breathed a sigh of relief. Little did he know, at that time, that he was talking to a young fellow who would be named a first-team All-American fullback and, later on, an NFL All-Star linebacker. Add to that list a number of head coaching accomplishments that stand to this very day. Once again, that's another story well worth sharing.

And Pardee subsequently learned, upon his arrival at Texas A&M, that his clothing wardrobe would consist of military uniforms, top to bottom. Surprise, surprise.

Suffice it to say that Coach Graves was delighted when Pardee arrived on campus. Subsequently, when Bryant's plane from Kentucky touched down at Easterwood Airport in January 1954, he already knew he had a great hire in Willie Zapalac. And Zapalac was credited with recruiting Jack Pardee, who proved to be an anchor for Coach Bryant's Junction Boys teams.

Here's an important fact to place firmly on the record. Because Pardee played six-man football, he was more than familiar with playing both offense as a fullback and defense as a linebacker. Pardee loved to deliver a blow almost as much as he enjoyed the challenge of shrugging off a well-delivered blow from an opponent.

One vignette seems worth mentioning. In Pardee's senior year the Texas A&M team found themselves facing the arch-rival Texas Longhorns on their home field, Memorial Stadium in Austin. That "hex," if you will, extended back thirty-three years. Every trip, up until then, ended with a Texas A&M loss. Texas A&M had never won a game before in Memorial Stadium.

The teasips, as they were known by the Corps of Cadets on the Aggie campus, were a solid team, led by Walter Fondren, a superb running back from Houston. And it was, by all descriptions, one helluva fine football game. Roddy Osborne, who was the starting quarterback for that game, led the Aggies down the field on their first possession. That march measured 72 yards in length, and John David Crow ran the last 27 yards with a dash that seemed to allow every Longhorn to try to tackle him. Each failed.

At the end of the first half, the Aggies went to the locker room to regroup, leading Texas 20-14.

The second half found the Longhorns kicking to the Aggies. Jack Pardee fielded the kickoff in the end zone and, instead of taking a knee, set sail for the other end of the field—right up the middle. The downfield blocking was what might best be described as textbook, and Pardee rambled and rumbled the length of the field. Pardee was not a sprinter. And as he neared the Longhorns' goal line, the Texas quarterback, Joe Clements, closed ground as Pardee's gas tank began to empty. The tackle was made short of the goal line, but—after quickly regrouping—Pardee was allowed to hammer his way into the Longhorns' end zone.

The Aggies won the first half. And they won the second half, too, beating the Texas Longhorns 34-21 and ending the dreadful Memorial Stadium hex. What makes the victory even more meaningful is the fact that the game was played both ways, and that required each and every player on the team—for both teams—to play at his very best.

Those who were there on that day—and there simply aren't many still walking around to share their memory of that special day in Austin late in November 1957—call this the very best football game they ever witnessed. Texas A&M won the Southwest Conference football championship in Coach Paul Bryant's third season.

But thanks to Jess Neely at Rice, there would be no trip to the Cotton Bowl. That, too, is another story.

Chapter 8

But Can Pardee Lead?

It was early in 1955 when Coach Bryant first expressed some concern to Smokey Harper about Jack Pardee's potential role as a team leader. Fresh in their memories was the preseason training camp in Junction where far more left than stayed. That trial-by-fire experience in Junction preceded a disappointing year for the Texas Aggies varsity team. They won but one game while losing nine.

The Texas Aggies had a pretty decent baseball team in 1955, and as the season was nearing an end, the Aggies closed out the SMU Mustangs and clinched a Southwest Conference baseball championship, the first in thirteen years. The victory was even sweeter because two Aggie football players played in that game. Joe Schero and Joe Boring were both in the lineup on that day.

One final game was on the schedule. It was an away game in Austin against the Texas Longhorns, who traditionally owned SWC baseball. The game was a weekday afternoon contest, and there was an immediate groundswell for supporting the team by filling the stands in Billy Disch Stadium with Aggies, who risked punishment for skipping class to attend the game.

Dr. David Morgan, who was then Texas A&M's president, issued an unofficial memo in which he reminded one and all that it was not possible to grant a one-day furlough from class and thus students should attend class, but only if it was a critical class that might have a major exam scheduled. Basically, the message was "Take your chances, and don't scream if your professor doesn't follow baseball."

As a result, that weekday afternoon game found the sizable crowd of 4,000 clad mostly in maroon and white. The teasips were nowhere near that motivated, so the Aggie contingent held a substantial audience advantage. Many of the members of the Texas A&M varsity football team made the trip to follow and show their support for teammates Boring and Schero.

It was about the middle of the game when a cluster of Texas Longhorn football players began to exchange catcalls with a slightly larger contingent of Texas Aggies footballers. The Longhorn guys were seated in a group a few rows down from the Aggies.

This story was recently confirmed by Roddy Osborne, who was seated at the end of one row when the UT All-SWC lineman, Buck Lansford, started tromping up the stairs to shut down the upstart Aggies, who were matching the tossing of insults in both directions.

As Lansford passed Osborne, he swung a mighty paw at Osborne and knocked him flying to the row below. But Pardee, who was seated close to Osborne, rose to the occasion and landed a bunch of punches on Lansford, who was then learning the lesson to be learned from attempting to fight someone while climbing up a flight of stairs.

Immediately more fights broke out, and a few blows were landed before the police arrived and restored order. It seems there were some arrests made, but all participants were released if they promised to behave and enjoy the rest of the game.

Enjoy it they did. The Aggies won 7-4 and Schero was credited with one hit. This all took place about eight years after the beginning of the College World Series at the end of the baseball season. At Texas A&M there was spring football, and the optimism was running high because the '54 fish football team had won the SWC freshman football championship and those young Aggies were on course to make a substantial improvement in the 1955 season.

Later on, Pardee and Lansford became teammates when they both played for the Los Angeles Rams. They enjoyed telling and retelling the story about that memorable day in Austin. By agreement, it could be presumed, they swapped off on their recollections of who had the upper hand.

The day after that game in Austin, Smokey Harper popped into Coach Bryant's office under the stands in Kyle Field and told the coach he had nothing to worry about insofar as Jack Pardee was concerned. Pardee knew how to hit, and he certainly knew how to lead.

Now let's fast-forward to the Texas A&M football game against the Baylor Bears that fall on Kyle Field. Texas A&M and Baylor didn't like each other.

Realize that this was a long time ago, during the period that folks now characterize as "back in the day." That's just the way it was back in the mid-1950s. Dwight D. Eisenhower was president, and Rick Perry, who would later become governor of Texas, was then seven years old.

It would be both inappropriate and inaccurate to label the Baylor Bears a dirty team, but their guys did tend to trash-talk a lot and typically taunted the Aggies more than the other members of the Southwest Conference fraternity, with the exception—of course!—of the Austin teasip frat boys.

Those Old Army Aggies really bristled when the Baylor clan chanted "Poor Aggies!" The Bears frequently hit late, and invariably there would be mischief in post-play pileups. The officiating crews would typically watch both the Aggies and Bears carefully as a means of keeping the game under control.

On this particular day, the then-undefeated Baylor Bears seemed to go out of their way to show their disdain for their closest SWC rival. They were noisy, to say the very least. On the other hand, Jack Pardee was a quiet guy. One of the Aggies' starting quarterbacks observed, "Pardee was typically a very quiet guy in the huddle. Coach Bryant insisted the on-field quarterback be fully in charge of the huddle. Jack rarely said anything."

Pardee didn't say a lot, but his on-the-field actions spoke volumes. He was not a profane fellow, either. His parents taught him better when he was growing up. Thus, there came a time in that 1956 A&M-Baylor game when Pardee was sitting on the sidelines during the first half. Ken Hall had received the starting nod at fullback. Pardee had been injured either in the preceding game or in the preceding week's practice.

Actually, Pardee did not sit much at all. Instead, he fidgeted and roamed around the sidelines, always quite close as he nervously shadowed Coach Bryant.

The Aggies knew they were in a real battle that day. The score was knotted at 6-6 at the half. Pardee had a well-known habit of shrugging his shoulders—as if his pads didn't quite fit—but that also probably indicated his increasing, itching desire to get back out on the field. It was still early in the third quarter, as Roddy Osborne recalls it, when Pardee suddenly popped into the huddle. He looked Osborne right in the eye and demanded, "Give me the fucking ball!" And that is precisely what Osborne did.

Osborne was responsible for calling the plays, but he also sensed Pardee was fired up and ready to take charge. The next three straight plays were power runs off the Aggies' left tackle, Charlie Krueger. The Aggies on the field sensed most of the air, and a lot of the fight on the part of the Bears had suddenly disappeared.

This occurred in the third quarter and was a key element in a 95-yard march downfield and into the Bears' end zone. The final play of the drive was a 4-yard plunge—by Jack Pardee over left tackle. However, the game was far from over. Both teams slugged it out—toe to toe—in a back-and-forth contest. Late in the fourth quarter John David Crow put the cap on a 63-yard drive with a 2-yard touchdown plunge.

The final score was 19-13 in the Aggies' favor. The Baylor Bears were no longer undefeated. Six personal fouls were called in the game. Truly it was a battle between two rivals that simply didn't like each other.

One casualty of the game was Kenneth Hall, who never played another down in a Texas A&M uniform. And that, in itself, is another story altogether.

Chapter 9

Recruiting, 1954

John Gilbert was a member of the Class of '58 and a superb player on three of Coach Bryant's four varsity teams—first as a member of the SWC championship (fish) team and thereafter as a letterman on the varsity teams. Gilbert was truly an outstanding player and a great role model for his younger teammates.

He shared his reflections on his recruitment in his Class of '58 yearbook, *Then and Now*. As Gilbert relates, it was a warm spring evening in 1954 in his hometown of Russellville, Arkansas. He was enjoying a malt with his girlfriend, Nancy, at the local Dairy Queen, which was then a drive-in. A neighbor stuck his head in the car window and told him he had a visitor at home who wanted to talk to him.

The family had no phone, so they made the five-mile drive out to the country where he lived. Upon his arrival, he found a tall, soft-spoken man in a brown felt hat and suit. It was none other than Elmer Smith, who had been signed on as an assistant coach by Coach Bryant.

Smith was a superb recruiter, and his territory included both Arkansas and Louisiana. Smith played a huge role in recruiting John David Crow, and he was probably the guy who lured Bobby Marks and Don McClelland from Louisiana. Those two guys were exceptional wide receivers. Smith explained to Gilbert that Texas A&M was an all-male, mostly military school in College Station, Texas.

Gilbert knew about Coach Bryant's reputation and recognized him to be an up-and-coming coach, so he was definitely interested. He also knew he needed a scholarship to be able to attend college. He recalled asking Coach Smith how long he had to make a decision.

And Coach Smith said, "You have fifteen minutes before I must leave." At the age of seventeen, Gilbert made the second-most important decision in his life: he signed on to become a Texas Aggie. The first and most important decision was to marry Nancy, who proved to be his life partner. They are still happily married and living in close proximity to the Texas A&M campus.

About that same time, similar recruiting stories were being played out in approximately 120 other homes in New Mexico, Louisiana, Mississippi, Oklahoma, Alabama, Kentucky, West Virginia, and Texas. All of those young players first reported to Walton Hall—then the athletic dorm right across from Northgate on the Texas A&M campus—and enjoyed making new friendships with their fellow recruits. As the young players were getting acquainted, a big upperclassman with "Hollywood good looks" approached the group and invited them to let him show them the ropes.

That first hard workout proved to be a memory they would never forget. Compared with those in high school, it was brutal. But everyone survived and felt pretty good about the first impression they had made with that big, handsome varsity dude. At least everyone thought he was a varsity guy.

But when the first official practice began, the handsome guy was nowhere to be seen. A few days later the young players were surprised to see Mr. Hollywood working out on another part of the field, where he found himself competing with the lowly Scout Team. The problem was, he couldn't even hold his own with the Scout Team, so he soon left the team.

A couple of years later, he popped up once again, to everyone's surprise. An assembled group of players was gathered in the Walton Hall lounge, where they were focused on a new TV series called *Bronco Lane*. The main character, Bronco, was showing tremendous courage, trekking across the desert to rescue a fair maiden. It was then they recognized Bronco Lane was none other than their Scout Team dropout, Ty Hungerford, who was destined to become the nation's newest western hero, hence and forevermore to be known as Ty Hardin.

There was much hootin' and hollerin' when the guys read his studio bio, which said he was an outstanding football talent at Texas A&M before a serious knee injury prematurely ended his football career. The simple truth was—as everyone knew—he flunked out when he couldn't compete with the Scout Team. One of the wags wondered just when it was he learned to "suck 'em up." Riding horseback while shooting a sixgun into the air was challenging, but it was nowhere near as tough as participating in the "Nutcracker Drill." More on that topic later.

About the time Hardin skedaddled for Rodeo Drive, the young Aggies were assembled at Walton Hall one evening when two school buses pulled up. Somewhere around thirty young men somberly filed out of the buses. One guy identified this as the varsity coming back from a place called Junction, where they had "survived" preseason practice. Far more quit than returned.

When the Junction stories began to be told, all of those young Aggies immediately understood. Needless to say, those stories stimulated a great deal of Oh-my-God fear in the recruits. One story, alluded to earlier, is certainly worth retelling here in a bit more detail.

Coach Bryant had a theory about quitting: "The first time you quit, it's hard. The second time, it gets easier. The third time, you don't even have to think about it."

That theory came into sharp focus at Junction. Suffice it to say the practices at Junction were very, very difficult. The practice field was devoid of grass. On this day that shall live in infamy, the Aggies' very best lineman, center Fred Broussard, arguably the best player on the team, suddenly decided he had endured quite enough criticism from Coach Bryant and the other coaches. Broussard was a big guy, but he strolled to the sidelines to ponder his dilemma. After a short spell, he went back onto the field and sought to rejoin the huddle. He asked Coach Bryant if he could rejoin the scrimmage.

Coach Bryant's answer was, "You just quit. You are no longer on this team."

Make no mistake about it. Broussard was a talented football player, but he didn't perform to Coach Bryant's standards. It's only fair to point out, however, that he later excelled as a lineman in the NFL.

Back to Junction. Following his pronouncement, Coach Bryant then looked over the remaining players on the field and asked if any of them had every played center in high school.

Troy Summerlin was then the "ranking" head football manager, and he had indeed played center in high school. Coach Bryant told him to immediately suit up and get ready to play. Summerlin weighed but 150 pounds. Summerlin stayed on the team throughout the fall schedule, but he was never forced into action. Meanwhile, that very evening, the defrocked Aggie center packed his bag and hitched a ride back to the Greyhound bus station for the trip back to College Station.

This was one of the first stories that made its way back to the freshman recruits. Coach Bryant also utilized a colorful way of phasing precisely how he felt about "quitters": "Once a turd, always a turd." Translated, that meant that the very idea of quitting represented a slippery slope.

At the time, freshmen players practiced together as a team for the most part. The preseason training rules had recently been changed, and freshmen were not allowed to practice more than thirty miles away from campus. Thus, all of those new freshman were spared the rigors of Junction. But everything was about to change.

Coach Bryant's first season in Aggieland was about to begin. Freshman were evaluated and a team roster was published each day designating a "color" for each player. Colored slipover vests were provided, and each player was expected to report to a certain practice sector. Those colored jerseys indicated which team a player was on: first, second, third, fourth, and Scout. Everyone wore the same basic practice uniform. Only the vests changed as a player moved up or down on the squad. The fish team was mostly coached by upperclassmen, who would probably be known as GA's—that's graduate assistants—in today's lingo.

After the first official practice for the new recruits, a small group of young players assembled at a place called Uncle Ed's—or maybe it was Uncle Jim's. Everyone ordered a Lone Star, which cost twenty-five cents those days. When the beer came, Loyd Taylor asked Jimmy Wright if he drank a lot of beer in high school back in Edinburg.

Jimmy, that wild and crazy guy, picked up his Lone Star, put his thumb over the bottle top, and bragged while saying, "Yeah, we drank a lot!"

A moment later, Jimmy turned beet red when the table and all of his pals were soaked with beer. That was just the first beer for most of the guys and just the first story worthy of retelling. That all took place sixty-five years ago. Time flies when you don't really want it to.

Chapter 10

Foresighted in Aggieland

As the high school football season was ending in the fall of 1953, the majority of the major college football coaches across the Southeast recognized there was a running back who excelled at Louisville's St. Xavier High School and who would fit in almost anywhere he chose to play. Actually, there were two stud running backs in Louisville. The first was a fellow by the name of Paul Hornung, but he came from a fine Catholic family and so he was destined to attend Notre Dame and not Kentucky. He ultimately won the Heisman Trophy, and reportedly the pope was thrilled.

But this story is about Bobby Nichols, not Paul Hornung. Young Nichols was a Kentucky guy, born and bred. Coach Paul Bryant's Kentucky Wildcats were rock-solid, but in need of yet another stud running back to assure their continued success. Coach Bryant and Nichols's high school coach were good friends—truly good coaching pals who talked to each other a lot, both on the phone and in person.

Nichols recently revealed that his high school coach first learned of Bryant's plan to leave Kentucky and move to "someplace else" months ahead of his actual departure. But the coach honored Bryant's request for secrecy inasmuch as his final "move" decision had not yet been made. When Nichols's high school coach first told Bryant about Nichols, the deal was immediately done. Bryant offered—and, through Nichols's high school football coach, Nichols accepted—a football scholarship to Kentucky.

Tragically, Nichols, along with some other lame-brained high school pals, was involved in a horrific automobile accident resulting from a 100-mph joy ride during the spring semester of his senior year. He suffered serious injuries, including a broken pelvis, concussion, back injury, and other internal injuries. He was hospitalized ninety-six days. Nichols's legs were also paralyzed for about two weeks, but he was ultimately able to regain full use of his legs after intensive physical therapy.

While all of this was occurring, Coach Bryant accepted the head football coaching job at Texas A&M. The way Coach Bryant saw it, "a deal is a deal." And so through Nichols's high school coach, Bryant offered a full-ride scholarship to Texas A&M. It was then that Nichols first learned about Texas A&M and its all-military regimen—and no coeds.

At this juncture, it is both important and relevant to mention that Bobby Nichols was a darned good amateur golfer. One of the best in Kentucky, that's for sure. It also seems reasonable to assume that Coach Bryant considered Nichols a fighter who might ultimately recover and would then be welcomed as a new member of the Fightin' Texas Aggies football squad. Could it be Bryant perceived Nichols was an even better fighter than he was either a running back or a golfer?

Nichols later admitted he knew very little about Texas A&M and College Station. However, he quickly accepted the scholarship offer and made plans to move to Texas. He recovered from his injuries and found himself a member of the Texas A&M golf team. He was truly an outstanding golfer, a big hitter, for sure. Nonetheless, the recovery was both long and arduous.

Bobby Nichols is probably the only athlete who has ever been accorded the distinction and privilege of holding a combined golf and football scholarship from Texas A&M. Up to that time, Texas A&M was usually an also-ran in the highly competitive Southwest Conference golf schedule. The nearby University of Houston—although not a member of the SWC—had a premier program with many young college players destined for a career in the PGA. The Longhorns, Baylor, and Arkansas were always tough to beat on the links. All that was about to change.

Nichols ultimately anchored two highly successful golf squads that finished in second place in both the 1957 and 1958 campaigns in the Southwest Conference. And Nichols was the No. 1–rated SWC golfer. Upon graduation, Nichols quickly progressed from the PGA's Q School to qualify for play as a professional in the PGA.

His career began in 1960. He ultimately recorded twelve victories during a stellar career. His best year was 1974, when he won twice, earned $124,747, and finished fourteenth on the money list. By today's standards, that sum probably appears to be miniscule. But back then it was serious coin.

By this time, of course, the Aggie Nation had come to realize that Nichols was one of "our guys" and even though Arnold Palmer had "Arnie's Army," Nichols had an Aggie Army to call his own. One can only imagine what other players thought when Nichols sank a long putt and a batch of Aggie pals in the gallery suddenly let out a loud "Whoop!"

The 1964 PGA championship was played at the Columbus Country Club in Columbus, Ohio. Nichols won that event with a final score of 271. That was three shots ahead of Arnold Palmer and defending PGA champion Jack Nicklaus. And Columbus was Nicklaus's home town. Nichols came oh-so-close to winning the Masters in 1967, finishing second to his lifelong friend, the late Gay Brewer.

Unfortunately, on Friday, June 27, 1975, Nichols—along with Jerry Heard and Lee Trevino of Dallas—was struck by lightning as their threesome stood under a large tree waiting out a passing thunderstorm during the Western Open. All three eventually came back to play, but the lightning severely damaged the nerve endings in Nichols's hands and fingers and greatly affected his ability to excel with both his short game and his putting.

Most golfers, including PGA professionals, never score a hole in one, but Bobby Nichols recorded twelve in his professional career.

Looking back, one cannot help but wonder just what it was that triggered Coach Bryant's quick response when he offered Nichols a second full scholarship while Nichols was still hospitalized, in traction, and facing the probability of months of arduous physical therapy. Bryant must have perceived that Nichols was not a quitter.

Here's a revealing quote attributed to Coach Bryant: "I have always tried to teach my players to be fighters. When I say that, I don't mean put up your dukes and get into a fistfight over something. I'm talking about facing adversity in life. There is not a person alive who isn't going to have some awfully bad days in their lives. I tell my players that what I mean by fighting is when your house burns down and your wife runs off with the drummer, and you've lost your job and all the odds are against you, what are you going to do? Most people just lie down and quit. I want my people to fight back."

Nichols is now leading a quiet, private life in Fort Myers, Florida. And he recalls the numerous times when Coach Bryant drafted him to play as his partner in celebrity Pro-Am golf tournaments. Their friendship proved to be both mutually beneficial and rock-solid. And don't you wonder what those guys competing against Coach Paul Bryant must have felt when they realized Coach Bryant had his own personal ringer? You gotta love having a partner who can hit a ball the length of three football fields laid end to end.

The entire Texas A&M football team during the Bryant era considered Nichols to be truly one of their very own. Bobby Nichols was a legitimate cardholder in the long list of athletes who played active roles during what became known as the Bryant era.

Chapter 11

Roddy Osborne

Mr. Versatility

If a Texas kid loves playing basketball and hangs around the gym or playground every day, honing his basketball skills with his pals, he is typically called—even affectionately!—a "gym rat." I do not honestly know what sort of a tag a young Texas fellow who loves playing football with the same intensity and dedication would be called, but if you were hanging around the football fields in the early 1950s in Gainesville, Texas, there is one lad who would have probably grabbed your attention and earned a suitable label.

He was Roddy Osborne. Still is. Not that long ago, he confessed he started playing serious organized football when he was still in elementary school. And he was a good player. Those days, when the guys would select buddies to play on their team, Osborne was usually one of the first selected. Coaches who kept an eye on those unsupervised scrimmages recognized Osborne's talent. Those who played against him knew firsthand about his abundant talents.

What was it exactly that set him apart? Well, Osborne liked to hit. He enjoyed dishing it out and definitely relished his ability to absorb a blow and keep right on playing. Truth be told, there are many youngsters who *think* they want to play football right up to the time when they find themselves on the receiving end of a well-executed block or a crushing tackle. Bruises and visible signs of on-field combat were seen as badges of honor.

During that particular time, Duffy Daugherty was beginning his impressive career at Michigan State University. He is credited with coining this memorable reminder: "Football is a collision sport. Dancing is a contact sport."

During the time when Osborne had progressed through elementary school to junior high school football, he had managed to gain well-deserved recognition for those latent skills. For each successive age group, he was ranked and rated as a top performer, an all-star for his age group who even went so far as to surpass those in classes higher than his class.

Back then, a kid's talent determined when and where he would play in any game. Kids who were really good played both offense and defense. Some did not. Since Osborne preferred to play defense, his skills allowed him to roam all over the field, and without ongoing contact with the sideline, he knew he could try to find the weak spot in the offensive scheme and wreak havoc. Today he would probably be called a rover, and that particular attribute is probably what caught Texas A&M's eye.

By the time Osborne took the field at Gainesville High School, that particular school was at the uppermost pecking order of statewide high school football programs. The Gainesville Leopards were fierce competitors against larger, more affluent schools like McKinney, Lewisville, and even Plano. Gainesville competed in a tough conference loaded with North Texas talent. Those were the kids destined to become future Southwest Conference starters.

One fellow who was one class higher than Osborne's was Chuck Curtis, who first competed with Osborne for the Leopards' quarterback position. Curtis eventually starred at Texas Christian as a quarterback. The taller Curtis was a superb passer, and Osborne's passing abilities fell short of superb. In truth, even though they competed vigorously against each other, they were also friendly teammates. That friendship disappeared the moment they found themselves facing each other across the line of scrimmage.

Osborne absolutely lived for those moments when he had the opportunity to lay the wood on his old high school buddy. Fast-forward to the A&M vs. TCU games, when Curtis was starting quarterback, for immediate, visible proof. Osborne was a superb both-ways player. Curtis's defensive skills paled in comparison to Osborne's.

The Gainesville Leopards were capably coached by Ed Dusek, a proud member of the Texas A&M Class of '45. That name is familiar to Old Army Aggies because they later witnessed Ed's son Brad performing at a high level on Kyle Field as a member of the Class of '73.

Osborne theorized that he was probably not heavily recruited by other SWC schools because of Dusek's allegiance to Aggieland. Any kid who was a promising performer for the Gainesville Leopards was probably destined for Texas A&M. But Chuck Curtis probably had purple blood coursing through his veins.

Osborne earned the focused attention of Phil Cutchin, the position coach for the Aggies' backfield, who followed Coach Bryant to A&M when he left Kentucky. Cutchin was a stellar quarterback for the Wildcat teams in the 1940s. Serious Kentucky followers recall Cutchin as the quarterback who preceded George Blanda and Vito "Babe" Parilli. It was Parilli who quarterbacked the Wildcats to victory over the Oklahoma Sooners in the 1950 Sugar Bowl. That win gave the Wildcats the opportunity to proclaim their team the unofficial national champion.

But back to Osborne. The word was out that Gainesville's Osborne belonged on the "gotta get" list. Cutchin, who recruited North Texas, learned from many in that part of the state that Osborne was a hitter. He absolutely loved to hit.

That did it. When Osborne finally signed his SWC letter of intent, he found himself on a roster of high school backfield talent that no other SWC team could even begin to match. It might also be said that it was the top group of running backs in the entire country.

True, the University of Texas was not that far behind, but that was not usually the case. The Longhorns could afford to sign every Texas athlete who might someday play for Texas. They would recruit and sign kids who would ride the bench for all four years. Most would never play a down. Most would be rewarded with the opportunity to dress for a varsity game. But during the week, they served as cannon fodder for the Longhorns' varsity teams.

And so Osborne found himself surrounded by an impressive group of young, talented football players when he arrived at Walton Hall in late August 1954. He was a candidate for a backfield position and facing a future Heisman Trophy in John David Crow. No less imposing was Kenneth Hall, then known coast to coast as the Sugar Land Express. All Hall did was post high school rushing records that still stand to this very day. Hall once ran for 520 yards in a single game! He toted the pigskin eleven times and *averaged* 47 yards per carry against Lutheran High School. Hall rarely played in the second half of any game in his senior season.

There is more. In that same game, he returned a punt for 82 yards, made a kickoff runback of 64 yards, and he then snatched a 21-yard interception for a combined 687 total yards. All this from a strikingly handsome young athlete who was faster than greased lightning.

After Crow and Hall, there were proven performers like Ed Dudley, the "Bull of the Pampas" and Loyd Taylor, the top running back in New Mexico, Carlos Esquivel, Bill Dendy, Bobby Joe Conrad, Donnie Grant, Don Watson, and Luther Hall. Each and every one of those guys was good enough to start for any school in the Southwest Conference.

Osborne realized the competition was going to be brutal. He weighed only 155 pounds, but that was 13 pounds more than Loyd Taylor.

Osborne said there was one specific play that fish team season that probably earned him a spot on the team with Coach Bryant. It was early in the season—perhaps against Baylor?—when a Cubs running back attempted a wide sweep and was first met by Taylor, playing as a corner back, who managed to hang on to one leg and impede the guy's forward movement.

Osborne, playing middle linebacker, was already running full speed for fifteen yards. A perfect hit: dead center. The Cub's helmet went flying, and they carried the fellow off the field on a stretcher. The next day, as the game field was played for the assembled team, Bryant played that one play again and again and expressed a strong desire to play anyone in the room who would make a tackle just like Osborne did on that Baylor kid.

The talented lad from Gainesville was also quick. That made him an excellent candidate for quarterback in Bryant's run-oriented offense. Osborne could move quickly down the line of scrimmage in either direction and, after reading the defensive end's response, either tuck the ball and cut inside or flip the ball to the trailing back for a run around end.

But he much preferred to hit over being hit. His versatility afforded him chances to play every position—except on the line—on both sides of the line of scrimmage.

The only thing he enjoyed more than hitting was simply competing as if his life depended on it, which also made Osborne a winner in Coach Bryant's eyes.

Chapter 12

The Sugar Land Express

In the early 1950s Charles Kenneth Hall was known, from coast to coast, as the Sugar Land Express. Hall was the fabled "All World" running back for the Sugar Land Gators, a bedroom community southwest of Houston that was much, much smaller way back then than it is now.

Hall was voted most handsome by his high school class. His girlfriend, Gloria, whom he later married, was class valedictorian. Hall graduated third. He was a squeaky-clean kid. His high school coach, Dugan Hightower, once said, "He wouldn't say 'shit' if he stepped in it."

On the football field he was hell on wheels. The Gators were a single-wing team, and Hall excelled as both a quarterback and a running back. And boy, howdy, did he ever excel! Those who followed him at that time, so very long ago, recall that he broke virtually all of the national rushing records and set marks that still stand, all while rarely playing in the second half. He was, by far, the top-rated running back in Texas, if not nationally. And he was probably the very first Texas recruit target deserving Coach Paul Bryant's rapt attention as he headed toward College Station early in 1954. Hall and Crow were in the same league, talent-wise.

It should be noted, for historical purposes, the simultaneous arrival on the recruiting scene of one Walter Fondren, who escalated from Houston's 5-A state champion Lamar Redskins to the University of Texas. Fondren was an All-State running back who took many of his teammates with him to Austin. Ed Price, then the Texas head football coach, was both thrilled and delighted with his 1954 freshman squad.

But Fondren had been cloaked in orange and white gear since his elementary school days, so his migrating to Austin was something of a foregone conclusion. In addition, four of his Houston Lamar Redskins teammates added depth to an already deep Longhorn squad.

Nonetheless, it is truly surprising to realize so many of Hall's rushing records stand to this very day in 2019. His career high school rushing record of 11,232 yards stood until surpassed in 2012. In his senior season he was credited with 4,045 yards. His record of thirty-eight games gaining more than 100 yards was not broken until the mid-1980s by none other than Emmitt Smith. Hall finished his prep career with 14,558 yards of total offense (11,232 rushing / 3,326 passing).

The stunningly handsome young athlete stood six feet one and weighed 195 pounds. According to the National High School Sports Record Book, Hall still holds multiple single-season records, including averaged points per game (32.9), touchdowns per game (4.8), and rushing yards per game (337.1).

Reread that last paragraph and let it sink in.

The last statistic is relevant in that he rarely played defense. The Gators did not want to risk injuring their prize running back, so he played only on offensive downs.

Hall was warmly received when he arrived on the campus in College Station. He was a personable, level-headed fellow and quickly earned respect and admiration from other classmates who also possessed considerable athletic skills. He was lights-out as a sprinter. Nobody could catch him!

When the Aggies fish team opened their season, Hall was the fullback and John David Crow and Loyd Taylor were the halfbacks. Bobby Joe Conrad was quarterback. But Jimmy Wright and Roddy Osborne were both close behind. Talk about competition!

The first time Hall carried the ball, he took it to the house with a 50-yard-plus carry. By season's end, Hall was the SWC's leading freshman scorer with 30 points—five touchdowns in five games—and he gained 206 yards on just twenty-six carries, averaging 7.9 yards per rush.

Unfortunately, Hall had zero experience on the defensive side of the line of scrimmage. As a halfback, he would have switched to a defensive back on defense. Fullbacks switched to linebacker, which would have been better for Hall, but he didn't really enjoy hitting the way a middle linebacker should, by Coach Bryant's standards.

Crow was quoted as saying, "Hall wasn't quite mean enough for Coach Bryant. Lord knows I loved Coach Bryant to death, but I'll say this—if Kenneth Hall had gone to play under someone like Bud Wilkinson at

Oklahoma, the world would have never heard much about John David Crow."

Midway through Hall's sophomore season, he grew tired of riding the bench and decided it was time to pack it up and take Highway 6 out of town. He went home to Sugar Land and married Gloria. Later on, there were reports that Hall felt Coach Bryant was not at all thrilled with Hall's marriage.

On the other hand, Crow was married and enjoyed a very close relationship with Bryant that those close to the program understood and acknowledged. Crow was a tough guy to handle, whether on offense or defense. Crow was a fighter.

Ed Dudley, Hall's roommate and one of a pack of talented backup running backs, had this to say about Hall:

> Kenneth was one of those easygoing kids who was never going to buck the system. Even when he was down and upset, I don't think it ever occurred to him to confront Bryant. If John David or I had the same kind of problems he had, we'd have probably been kicking Coach Bryant's door in and demanding some kind of explanation, then maybe taken a punch at him. Sadly, that wasn't Kenneth's style. He would walk away from the situation before he ever did anything like that.
>
> I knew it was not going to work for him at A&M and even went so far as to suggest he transfer to another school. Either that or forget football and concentrate on the decathlon. He was a cinch to make the Olympic team if he had worked at it. He was that kind of an athlete.

The truth was, Bryant wanted hard-nosed players who could play defense first and offense second. Hall was a stranger in the defensive backfield.

The late Jack Pardee was quoted as saying, "When I first saw Kenneth Hall on the practice field—a big guy (6′1″ and 195 pounds) who was lightning fast and had all of those other athletic skills—I figured I had just been demoted to second string."

Later that same year, Hall came to regret his decision and cried as he asked Coach Bryant to allow him to return for spring training. To his surprise, Coach Bryant accepted his apology and agreed. Hall's reinstatement opened the door for him to battle Pardee for the starting job at fullback. Hall's junior season was Pardee's senior season.

Tragically, Hall's junior season was more of the same. He became frustrated with the constant criticism dished out in practices. And he sat.

Then, against Baylor in the seventh game of the season, Bryant told Hall he would be the starter at fullback and just as Hall felt he was getting into a rhythm, he was suddenly pulled and found himself back on the bench. Pardee returned to the game, and Hall sat out the rest of the game. He later confessed it was that one defining moment that spurred the thought that maybe—just maybe—he didn't want to play football any more.

Off the field it was another story. He was ranked the No. 1 freshman cadet in his outfit. He was the star performer on the Texas Aggies track team. But the Aggies' coaching staff cared about only one thing: Ken Hall could *not* play linebacker. Defense was a foreign language to him.

A search of the historical records revealed there later came a time when Coach Bryant sent Hall a letter saying he felt bad about the way Hall was treated. Hall graciously responded "Don't worry. It's okay." He was simply that kind of a guy.

What happened next? Hall later shared this: "I knew it was time to back up and regroup. So, in 1957, armed with a $7,000 contract plus $700 for travel, I skipped my senior season and went to Canada to play for the Edmonton Eskimos."

For the season, he rushed forty-eight times for 376 yards; punted twenty-two times for a 41.2-yard average, and scored four touchdowns, one on a 73-yard punt return. But this was only Canada. In 1958 the Baltimore Colts picked Hall in the fourteenth round of the NFL draft. Those days, Unitas was calling the plays, and Hall seemed secure with a spot on the roster right up to the moment when Sam Huff flattened him. That tackle came in an exhibition game. Huff landed on Hall in such a fashion that it pushed his head down between his knees. That sixth vertebra in his neck was cracked in five places.

That injury ultimately caused him to hop from the Pittsburgh Steelers to the Chicago Cardinals and then on to the Houston Oilers. He once ran back a 104-yard kickoff return against the New York Titans. But he never came close to regaining his former ability to play football.

The Sugar Land Express finally chugged to a stop in Fredericksburg, Texas. There Hall owned and operated a barbecue place for a number of years in that beautiful Texas landmark town. Fredericksburg considers him to be one of its own. He and his wife, Gloria, relish their quiet life of retirement with nothing but fond memories of a wonderful career that will never be matched.

Kenneth Hall has been quoted as saying, "Coach Bryant says I am his biggest mistake. There is an honor in that."

Chapter 13

One-Armed and Dangerous

Hank Crisp—later Coach Hank Crisp—was one of Coach Paul Bryant's teammates at the University of Alabama. They were old friends. Coach Bryant valued their friendship and trusted Crisp's judgment.

Early in 1954 Crisp recommended that Coach Bryant send one of his assistant coaches to attend an Alabama high school All-Star game and that he look closely at a young talent by the name of Murry Trimble. Trimble was a rock-solid lineman who was tough, resilient, and fast. Coach Elmer Smith was dispatched to the scene, and his reports to Bryant back in College Station were all positive. Not only that—the youngster also played and excelled at varsity-level baseball and basketball!

Bryant was curious. If this young fellow was so darned talented, why hadn't some other college picked him up? That was the question he posed to Coach Smith, who said, "Well, Coach Bryant, Trimble only has one arm. The young fellow lost the lower part of his left arm—about halfway between the elbow and the wrist—in a childhood accident."

And then the light came on for Coach Bryant. Murry Trimble, destined to be known as "Stubby," had but one arm. The same was true for Hank Crisp! He was also missing his left arm. And so Murry Trimble—the pride of Hanceville, Alabama—found himself holding a scholarship offer to join a talented group of athletes at Texas A&M for the beginning of the Bryant era.

Trimble was anything but a "typical" guy. He hitchhiked from Alabama to College Station to begin his career as a Texas Aggie. And when there was a break on campus, he hitchhiked back to Alabama. Trimble marched to the beat of a different drum.

Trimble was welcomed by the new crop of recruits and quickly earned respect as he competed for a guard slot on the fish team. It didn't take that long for the fellows who lined up against him to wonder if that stub of an arm shouldn't be considered a dangerous weapon. In those days the helmets had a single gray bar or a clear plastic bar with just enough room to allow Trimble's stub of an arm to maul an opposing lineman's nose. Stubby knew how to use that nub.

One occasion comes to mind during a game against the Baylor Bears in Waco one night when Trimble, playing nose to nose with the Bears' All-SWC center, continued his practice of jamming his stub up and under the center's face guard. Apparently, the officials never really picked up on Stubby's transgressions.

Trimble played alongside a short, stout fellow by the name of Jim Langston, who hailed from Texas City. Coach Pat James first labeled Langston "Round Man," and the name stuck. Although Round Man was only about five feet six, he packed 195 pounds onto his stout frame. And he was as quick as a cat. Mean, too. Round Man knew the kind of punishment Trimble could dish out because he practiced against Trimble all the time.

Thus, Langston found it downright hilarious that the huge Baylor center was having his facial contours altered by Stubby Trimble.

Finally, the Baylor guy had had enough. After hearing Langston laugh once too many times, the Baylor guy looked left and right and then aimed a big fist at Langston's face. Langston ducked. The blow bounced off his helmet, and the Baylor center was ejected from the ballgame.

Actually, to be clear, Langston didn't laugh. He cackled. And as the Baylor fellow was escorted off the field of play, all he could hear was Langston cackling.

The 1956 Texas Aggies team included Murry "Stubby" Trimble, an All-SWC first team guard performer. Here's where the fun begins!

The following spring, a brand new, black Lincoln Continental suddenly showed up at Kyle Field. It was parked in Coach Bryant's reserved parking spot. Smokey Harper issued an order that we needed to find out who owned that car and get it moved before Coach Bryant arrived and all hell broke loose.

It didn't take that long for Stubby to show up and move his new car. It didn't take that much longer for the representatives from the Southwest Conference to show up on campus and demand an explanation from Trimble. The meeting was ominous. Trimble was the star witness on his own behalf and calmly explained the new car was a gift from his father, who he said had promised to buy whatever car Trimble wanted if he and his Texas A&M team both succeeded. I can vaguely recall that Trimble positioned his father as a man who was capable of purchasing a car. For cash. He had the bill of sale as evidence.

The kangaroo court that had so hastily assembled buckled under the weight of the evidence and accepted Stubby's reasoning that he should not be punished.

End of story? Well, sort of.

About ten years ago, in a long, hilarious conversation I had with Stubby back in Alabama, he told me the *real* story—in confidence. Sadly, that wild-and-crazy guy passed away not that long ago, and I feel honor-bound to keep his secret. I strongly suspect each and every surviving member of the three teams coached by Coach Bryant at Texas A&M has at least one Stubby tale to share. Some of them might be true!

Nonetheless, I found it very interesting to hear so many wonderful things about Trimble from his many friends in Alabama. Mike Cupp, a 2007 Cullman County (Alabama) Sports Hall of Fame inductee, played for Trimble on the inaugural team from Good Hope, Alabama, and maintained a lifelong friendship with Stubby. "He did so many great things. He was a great and incredible athlete. A so-called handicap for most people wasn't for him. Really, just a heck of a guy. Athletically, I don't know of anything he couldn't do. I really don't."

Trimble's brother, Wayne, played college football at Alabama through 1966—also for Coach Bryant at Alabama—before being drafted in the fourth round of the 1967 NFL draft as a cornerback.

Tough guys succeed during tough times, and Trimble was as tough as they come.

Chapter 14

How High Can a Frog Jump?

It was springtime in Aggieland when Fritzie Connally—then known to his classmates and upperclassmen as Frog Connally—was meandering across Kyle Field on the way to G. Rollie White Coliseum for basketball practice. Smokey Harper taped his ankles.

Coach Bryant called the Texas Aggies basketball team "thump thumps," and Smokey considered those players "*his* thump thumps." Others called them "round-ballers." Smokey felt attached to the "thump thump" athletes. Little did Frog know that, way back when, Smokey Harper was a two-way athlete as a younger man. Add to it the fact that Harper served as head basketball coach at Vanderbilt in the mid-1940s while World War II was winding down. He liked basketball almost as much as football. Besides, as head athletic trainer, he treated all Texas A&M athletes well.

This particular afternoon was in full-bloom springtime. The newly mown grass on Kyle Field was fragrant, just as it was around the MSC and all over the campus. Someone said it was spring when young men's thoughts turned to . . . what was it, basketball? Or perhaps track?

Frog Connally was a highly recruited basketball player who had done some pretty amazing things as a high schooler during his days at Thomas Jefferson High School in San Antonio. His talent was sufficient at that level to have attracted the attention of John Floyd, the first of three coaches under whom Fritzie ultimately played while at A&M. Although Fritzie could nail the jumper better than most, it was his wheels and his ability to leap high and snag rebounds that caught Floyd's attention. Floyd extended a grant-in-aid scholarship and welcomed Frog Connally at mid-term to a squad that developed to accomplish some pretty remarkable things during Fritzie's four years in Aggieland.

Fritzie and three other round-ballers left the training room under Kyle Field and, realizing they had a little time to burn before practice began, strolled over to the track team's practice area at the south end of Kyle Field. All of the basketball guys were wearing their fatigues over their practice uniforms. This is relevant, as they would later shed their fatigues when they arrived at courtside.

The high-jump pit was the focal point of their curiosity. As they watched, the track guys were honing their craft as they set about attempting to clear the bar, which was set at about six feet five. The US collegiate high-jump record at that time was but a fraction of an inch below seven feet.

Aggies being Aggies and the spirit of competition being what it has always been at Aggieland, some conjecture was entertained as to how difficult could it be to clear the present height of the bar. The round-ballers' fatigues were potentially a sartorial handicap, at the very least. And so it came to pass that, while the track guys watched and prepared to be amused at the round-ballers who had invaded their turf, the competition began. At stake was the pooled pocket change that each of the basketball dudes had in his pocket. The guy who cleared the bar first would win that money, which was anted up and stashed in one of the guy's baseball cap. Each succeeding jump—and failure—caused the gnashing of teeth and the shedding of yet another layer of the hindering outer wear and, although there were some close efforts, there was no cigar. The cash prize remained unclaimed.

Finally, clad only in his tee shirt and jockstrap, Frog Connally propelled himself speedily down the runway and launched himself headfirst, if you can imagine that kind of a jump for a frog, and cleared the bar and landed head first in the sand pit, which was the typical landing area at that point in time. Cushioned balloon landing pads were well down the road in the mid-1950s. Fritzie landed in about six inches of packed sand, and it was not a pretty sight.

The bar did not quiver because Frog Connally cleared it easily. Standing quietly by, observing in the background, was a person whose signature look was the color brown. Typically, he wore brown slacks and a brown fedora, which was then in style, and if he wore a sport coat, you could bet it would also be brown. Maybe a dark tan, but brown. You get the picture.

Although Connally did not know it at that time, his ad hoc performance was viewed by none other than Col. Andy Anderson, A&M's head track coach. Without much fanfare, Colonel Andy sidled up and asked Connally if he planned to go out for track that spring. Connally then revealed that his heart, first of all, belonged on the basketball court. And he was late for practice, so the conversation was ended.

However, when the springtime postseason basketball practices concluded, Coach Floyd told Connally to report to Coach Anderson's office as soon as possible. To Connally's surprise, Coach Anderson turned out to be the very same brown-clad fellow who witnessed his over-the-bar, off-the-wall performance not that many days ago. It might have been better described as an on-the-spot promotion.

Coach Anderson offered and Fritzie accepted a track scholarship, and although that first year's competition was against other first-year Southwest Conference participants, Fritzie competed and competed well. He placed high in varsity competition at the Texas Relays, the Kansas Relays, the Border Olympics, and other SWC track meets and earned the distinction of performing more than capably as a two-sport T-Association letterman, as it was then called.

History also reminds us that the rules of competition were subsequently revised, thanks perhaps to Fritzie's unorthodox and somewhat dangerous style of clearing the bar (almost) headfirst. Later in life, high jumpers cleared even loftier heights with either a style called the Eastern (or Western) Roll or, later, the Fosbury Flop, made famous by Dick Fosbury, who won a gold medal in the Olympics with his unique somersault style.

Furthermore, had Fritzie not risen to the challenge to clear that bar and win some cash in the process, he might never have met his future bride on that beautiful, long-remembered afternoon on Kyle Field. Here's that story.

During an invitational track meet at Kyle Field, Connally and another Aggie high jumper strolled over to the stands to check out the lovely ladies who had shown up to cheer on their respective schools. Two of the Sam Houston State coeds seemed more exceptional than the others, but although the introductory conversation was both brief and exciting, the meeting ended far too soon.

Shortly thereafter, in Huntsville, Connally and an Aggie pal attended an event many will remember fondly—Frontier Days—and Lady Luck stepped into the picture. Lo and behold, the same two girls appeared, as if by magic. They were roommates at Sam Houston State, as it was then called, and their names were Byrne and Beverly. Lovely ladies, too. Spring was still in the air.

And not that many months later, after many long letters, memorable dates, and countless phone calls, Fritzie proposed and Byrne said "Yes!" and way, way, way down the road in the spring of 2007, those two celebrated their golden wedding anniversary. Talk about a giant leap for Frog Connally!

Oh, yeah. One more tidbit. Beverly, whose nickname was Bevo, married Aggie footballer Charlie Krueger, and they also enjoyed many years together. There's more. Byrne and Fritzie had a son, also named Fritzie—but called Fritz—who broke virtually every high school baseball batting record while playing for Pasadena High School in 1976. Simply stated, Baylor wanted the young Fritz more than his father's Texas Aggies did, and that proved to be a decision A&M regretted deeply.

Fritz became one of the best sluggers to ever come through Baylor and led the Bears to two trips to Omaha. He was named All-SWC in all four of his years at Baylor. When he graduated, Fritz Connally was Baylor's all-time homerun hitter after racking up thirty-eight dingers in his career (now fifth on that list). He topped off a stellar college career in Waco and was drafted by the Chicago Cubs in 1980. He had an impressive minor league career and, during his short time on the Chicago Cubs roster, hit three home runs. Two were grand slams. Fritz Connally was ultimately inducted into the Pasadena ISD Athletics Hall of Fame, the Texas Athletic Hall of Fame, the Baylor Athletic Hall of Fame, and the Southwest Conference Hall of Fame.

Fritzie and Byrne Connally now reside on their ranch, not far from Kyle Field. Like so many from the Class of '58, he lives from one Texas Aggies football season to the next. Fritzie Connally was—and still is—a class act! Smokey Harper would have been so very proud to see what Frog Connally accomplished over a lifetime as a Texas Aggie.

Chapter 15

Team Photo Day

Jim Laughead was the go-to photographer-guy for every team in the Southwest Conference. He also took care of as many college teams as he could accommodate in both the Big 8 and the Southwest region, but it was tough to respond to so many schools in such a short period of time. Laughead was based in Dallas, and he spent virtually his entire career both planning and staging action shots for each team on their predetermined Team Photo Day. He had a nationally famous reputation.

Team Photo Day was that special day early in the fall training cycle when the team would suit up in their new game uniforms and spend almost the entire morning participating in staged publicity shots. Laughead coined the term "huck 'n' buck" to best describe his style. The team wore their new uniforms, and Laughead was decked out in his same old gear. As we all recall, that was a pair of blue coveralls and a wide-brimmed, floppy hat.

Laughead had developed special techniques for posing athletes to appear as if they were in action. Running backs would typically include at least one Heisman-styled stiff-arm pose, always running full tilt. And linemen would growl and yell and leap toward the lens as Laughead urged them to "Dig . . . dig . . . dig!" And they loved it.

It was early in the fall training preseason when the Texas Aggies football squad formed up in the practice area immediately behind the old Kyle Field. That same field, not that many years after, became a giant parking lot to accommodate the new Kyle Field's ever-increasing crowds. Typically, Jones Ramsey, who was then sports publicity director, would use this occasion to fully replenish his supply of stock photographs that were typically requested as graphic support for sports news features and stories. Ramsey's title eventually changed to sports information director, and today each major university has a staff dedicated to disseminating a constant flow of support information—photos and videos and stories for all media—but this was a time when all of those chores were handled by one man.

His office consisted of a desk, a typewriter, and a two-drawer filing cabinet. The printed stuff was in the top drawer; the booze was in the bottom drawer. In those days Jones would gladly supply the "fuel" to keep the news guys energized.

Ramsey both knew and appreciated Laughead's skills. Laughead's talents were typically displayed in national magazines, including *Sports Illustrated*, *Time*, and *Life*. Open any college or university book from that era, and you will undoubtedly see photos staged and shot, all from Jim Laughead's cameras. He passed away many years ago but left behind an impressive number of innovative, young photographers who tried ever so hard to emulate his style.

Team Photo Day was also the occasion for the coaching staff to break out their new gear, which included practice shirts, jackets, and caps. At that time the preferred style of headgear for the coaches was a white baseball cap with a solid maroon T. As best recalled, this was also a time before caps were offered with adjustable bands to allow for quick-fit resizing.

As I watched the action being filmed, I also became aware of the fact that each of the coaches was searching through a large box of caps to find a cap that fit. This entailed, obviously, trying on any number of caps to find the right one. Coach Bryant, I can vividly recall, had a cap perched atop his head that was, shall we say, way too small. It reminded me of one of the beanies that teasip frats wore.

Coach Bryant was not one bit happy. But this had nothing to do with me, so I was startled to suddenly hear him yell, "M-G-R!"—coach-speak for "Manager." Fact is, he would also frequently address student trainers as "M-G-R," but I do not ever recall any one of them who sought to correct him.

Coach Bryant had a large head, to say the very least, and Smokey Harper, as the Aggies' head trainer, probably was responsible for ordering the uniforms from the Dallas supplier. This was long before Nike and Adidas and so many others began to evolve as gigantic branding resources.

At any rate, I leapt to attention while Coach Bryant scowled and Smokey quickly explained to me that I needed to immediately grab the keys to one of the State of Texas / Texas A&M cars and head for Dallas. Double-time.

Pronto! But no speeding tickets. He made clear that I needed to be back on campus in time for the afternoon practice. Smokey assured me he would be in touch with the uniform supplier and make it crystal clear that they needed to provide me with an adequate supply of caps that would fit Coach Bryant.

To this very day, I can squint my eyes shut and recall that scene where Coach Bryant had a way-too-small cap on his head. And he was not happy. It reminded me of that saying about "Mama being happy," only altered to mean, "When Coach Bryant is unhappy, nobody better be happy."

I drove to Dallas wearing my practice shorts, a maroon tee shirt, and my cleats. It never even occurred to me to change before I departed. I knew the uniform supplier's location in Dallas, but I could only pray that Smokey had managed to connect with the company prior to my arrival. Thankfully, those fellows at the uniform company were eagerly awaiting my arrival and had cleared the shelves of *all* Texas A&M caps for my selection. For all I know, a team of uniform elves had hand-made a number of caps for this one brutally important occasion.

I made it back to campus late in the afternoon and prior to the start of practice. Coach Bryant and Smokey were there when I delivered the box of new caps. The very first cap Coach Bryant retrieved from the box fit him perfectly. To say that I was relieved would be a gross understatement. But to my great surprise, he turned to me and said, "M-G-R, thanks for taking care of this for me."

Of course, there came a time when Coach Bryant's headgear of preference became a gray, black, and white houndstooth fedora. He made that hat famous from coast to coast. But that's another story for another time.

Chapter 16

The Day the Rain Came Down

If you ask most any Texas Aggie who was on campus during the four seasons (1954–57) when Coach Bryant was prowling the Aggies' sideline about the most memorable game they ever witnessed on Kyle Field, the vast majority of them would say, "The Texas A&M–TCU game in 1956." This is a rather surprising revelation when you realize it wasn't the final game of that same season when the Aggies finally—finally!—broke the Memorial Stadium jinx in Austin with a 34-21 defeat of the Texas Longhorns.

To more accurately set the scene, there were blue skies right before the game began, and those same blue skies were present when the game finally ended. But in between, an incredible thunderstorm and possible tornado blasted through Kyle Field and simply flattened more than 100 airplanes on the ground across the campus at Easterwood Field. This was before there was AccuWeather, of course.

The later game against the Longhorns was the last game in an undefeated season that brought the Southwest Conference football championship to Texas A&M. Regrettably, the Aggies were denied the right of representing the SWC in the Cotton Bowl, a result of an SWC probation levied against the Bryant-led team, the third of the four he coached.

But the Texas A&M–TCU contest was the fifth game of that 1956 season, and the Aggies were undefeated at that juncture, with only a 14-14 tie with the Houston Cougars blemishing a perfect record. The Horned Frogs were seeking to avenge a painful loss in Fort Worth the previous year. TCU was projected to be the favored co-contender, along with the Aggies, for the Southwest Conference football championship. TCU was a team that was loaded with speed, talent, and desire. So were the Aggies.

As the time for the kickoff approached and the clouds began to darken, a packed Kyle Field crowd of 40,000-plus came to realize this was going to be a "piss pot and poncho" kind of a day that nobody would ever forget. The wind began to blow with a vengeance, and the rain didn't just fall—it blew *sideways* and swirled around and about Kyle Field for virtually the entire game. The on-field officials found it necessary to hold on to the ball until the center took control to start the play. It was widely reported that a tornado touched down nearby during the game, but that was a report that could never be personally verified. Everyone was at the game, you see.

Kickoffs were a challenge. Punting was impossible. An addled, designated Aggie captain miscalled the coin toss option, and that unlucky choice caused the Aggies to have to kick into the gale-force wind, which gave the Horned Frogs possession at midfield. And the series most remembered was when TCU players, with those same gale-force winds at their backs, ran eight straight plays right into the teeth and aimed at the heart of the Aggie defense. On their final try, the Frogs' outstanding quarterback, Chuck Curtis, lofted a pass to their rangy All-SWC end, O'Day Williams, and TCU grabbed a lead that held up until late in the fourth quarter. Nobody was surprised when the extra point failed. As the storm's intensity increased, so did the tempo of the game.

The previous year, the Aggies' versatile halfback, Don Watson, had hauled in a touchdown pass in the far corner of the end zone at Amon Carter Stadium in Fort Worth. That play broke both the heart and the back of the Frogs at the same time. Now, back at Kyle Field, "Frog-Killer" Watson, who weighed but 150 pounds soaking wet, toted the heavy leather on the Aggies' final scoring drive.

These were the days when players played both ways, if you will recall. And there was a wrinkle in the rule the long cigars worked in that said when a player left the field and was replaced by a substitute, that player could not return until the next quarter.

The series began, appropriately enough, when Watson, a defensive back when on defense, yelled "Bingo!" as he hauled in an errant Curtis pass that he snagged in the end zone and then scampered across the slick Kyle Field turf to the Aggies' 20. "Bingo!" was the word the Aggies yelled when they intercepted a pass.

As is so often the case where Texas weather is concerned, the winds began to die down and blue skies started to emerge as the clouds moved away. A good omen? Perhaps. From there, as the clock ticked down and nobody in Kyle Field dared take a breath, the Aggies used eight plays to march 80 yards for what proved to be the tying touchdown.

Crow started it off with a 21-yard dash behind superb blocking around end. Roddy Osborne kept for two on a QB keeper and, on the next play, executed a well-timed pitch to Watson, who rambled 37 yards to the TCU 20. Crow plunged for two more and then, on the next play, swept end again for 11 and a first down on the TCU 7.

Fearing another sweep, the hard-rushing TCU defensive unit realized, in the blink of an eye—too late!—that Watson had no intention of dashing around end. He pulled up as he saw Crow make his cut and neatly lofted the ball into Crow's waiting hands.

The officials signaled "Touchdown!" and every single eye in the stadium turned to watch the diminutive Loyd Taylor as he lined up for an extra point that was anything but routine.

However, Taylor calmly booted the ball through the uprights and then—only then—could everyone breathe a sigh of relief.

Aggies 7, TCU 6. End of game. Little did anyone know, at that time, that they had just witnessed a Texas A&M game that would be indelibly etched in their memories for the rest of their lives.

There is an interesting sidebar story that deserves to be told, and it happens to revolve around two Class of '58 teammates. At halftime, when the teams retired to their respective locker rooms, the decision was made that a change of jerseys was quite necessary. The rain and mud had so soiled the uniforms that the coaches simply couldn't tell who was who. Perhaps reflective of the fact that the late Barlow "Bones" Irvin was then director of athletics and a man who absolutely relished a miserly control over the Athletic Department budget, there was no second set of clean jerseys for each and every player. Bones never met a dollar he didn't like, or so it was said.

It was thus decided that a "jersey swap" was in order—not for everyone on the team, but for the starters. Mostly. One player who played well when he played but really didn't get to play that often was Bill Appelt, a tall end and one of Hallettsville's finest youngsters. Along with George Gillar, Appelt had transferred to Texas A&M from Victoria Junior College to be an Aggie. His No. 84 jersey was appropriated and given to none other than John David Crow. But there was a problem.

Nobody in the Humble broadcast booth learned of the jersey switch until it was too late. The late Kern Tips and Alec Chesser relished telling the story in the following months. And so, to the delight of a huge Southwest

Conference radio audience that reached every corner of the state of Texas, the unsung hero—Bill Appelt—came off the bench and led the Aggies to victory in a game nobody could ever forget.

Appelt, now retired, enjoys his life in his hometown of Hallettsville, and one of his most prized personal possessions is a sports story that appeared in his hometown newspaper chronicling his feats on Kyle Field that wild, stormy autumn afternoon. The story includes a photo of Appelt supposedly hauling in the pass from Watson that tied the game.

The victory was made even sweeter for Appelt when he was leaving the A&M locker room after the game and was enthusiastically met and hugged by none other than Les Appelt, who, although not directly related to Bill, was nonetheless one proud member of the Appelt clan. He, too, thought the feats of his perhaps-distant relative hero would never be forgotten.

The late Les Appelt, who gave generously to A&M over the years, delighted in telling everyone this same story. After all, No. 84 had his day. Didn't we all?

Chapter 17

He-e-e-re's Mickey Herskowitz!

Legendary sports journalist Mickey Herskowitz's first big coverage assignment for the *Houston Post*, which was then the morning newspaper in the Bayou City, was to serve as the assigned beat reporter for Texas Aggies. He and Coach Paul Bryant arrived on campus at about the same time, early in 1954. For the record, Herskowitz later joined the afternoon newspaper, the *Houston Chronicle*, when the *Houston Post* quietly folded.

Mickey was my idol as a sportswriter. We had both attended the now-gone San Jacinto High School in the Bayou City, and I avidly followed his coverage of the Aggies. We saw each other at almost every practice. Herskowitz is now retired and living in Houston, but he found time to share with me some of his Smokey Harper and Paul Bryant memories from that dim and distant past.

One afternoon as fall practice was under way, Jones Ramsey was escorting an older fellow around the practice field and waiting for a moment when he could introduce the special guest, Homer Norton, to Coach Bryant. As the practice was moving along, Smokey strolled over, and Jones, who was then the Aggies' sports publicity director, introduced the two.

Ramsey then mentioned the 1939 Texas A&M national championship team, and Smokey chimed in with this observation: "You know, we watched some of the game and practice films from that team back then to see what we could learn about them. And you know what? As sorry as those folks right out there on the practice field are right now, they could have beat that 1939 championship team."

After a short spell, Norton then quietly departed. And when Ramsey rejoined Smokey, Harper asked, "Hey, Jones, who was that nice fellow?"

Ramsey said, "Smokey, that was Homer Norton. He was the head football coach of that 1939 national championship team."

Smokey said, "Well, damn. My hearing aid was turned off, and I didn't hear a word anyone was saying. I think I need to get some new batteries."

You gotta love it. And there's more. Shortly after being hired as trainer at Vanderbilt University, some generous Commodore supporter gifted Smokey with an all-expenses-paid week in Miami. It might have been in conjunction with the Orange Bowl. Keep in mind, this was a long, long time ago. When Harper checked in at the Fontainebleau Hotel, he signed the registration form and showed his business as "Vanderbilt Trainer."

Not that long after his arrival, he began receiving fruit baskets and phone calls and invitations to special parties. One fellow even offered to send his limo over to pick him up. His phone was ringing off the wall. And he didn't know why.

Smokey finally shared this bit of surprising news with his benefactor. Smokey said, "You know, these are just the friendliest people I have ever met. What a fantastic welcome they have given me."

"Smokey," his benefactor explained, "these folks think you are the trainer for Vanderbilt Stables, and they're all seeking to learn tips from you about this Saturday's big racing event at Hialeah Race Park." The fabled Vanderbilt Stables had horses in virtually every race on the Saturday card. Inside knowledge was valuable, to say the least.

Herskowitz next recounted another Smokey Harper recollection that tied back to Texas A&M's Richard Gay. Gay was a superb athlete from Shreveport's Byrd High School and was remembered for his stellar participation as a junior when John David Crow was a senior at Springhill High School. That game ended in a tie in 1953 and was acclaimed as "the finest high school game ever played." Gay was the first All-American player from Byrd High School. He was a superb football player and may have been an even better performer in track and field.

What set Gay apart from most of the players at Texas A&M was his ability to excel as a linebacker. He was, without question, the best there was at Texas A&M since Jack Pardee. In a game against TCU, Herskowitz recalled, Gay was credited with seventeen unassisted tackles. That is a fantastic accomplishment even by today's standards.

We both recalled the Gator Bowl game Texas A&M played against the Tennessee Volunteers in 1958. The Vols were led by an All-American halfback named Johnny Majors. Tennessee eventually won the game, but the play most remembered was the second-half kickoff. Majors fielded the ball at the goal line and headed straight up the middle with excellent blocking ahead.

Someone missed blocking Gay, and he absolutely leveled Majors at about the 25 yard line. The crown of Gay's helmet hit Major's knee, and the impact knocked Gay out. Herskowitz recalls the crowd in the stadium became instantly deadly silent. The Vols had to assist Majors back to the bench to recover.

Gay also spent some time on the bench, but as the third quarter was nearing an end, Bryant yelled to Smokey to get Gay ready to retake the field. Gay hustled over, but someone had to retrieve his helmet.

When Gay saw the dished-in crown of his helmet, he fainted, dropping to the ground on the spot. And he was aided back to the bench to recover—again.

Both Gay and Majors did return, and although it was a hard-fought game, Coach Bryant's final game as head football coach at Texas A&M ended with the Vols winning, 3-0. The Texas Aggies lost the last three games coached by Coach Bryant by a total of six points.

Here's another story about Smokey. In a game against TCU and, once again, in the third quarter, Gay was shaken up in a play and Smokey went onto the field to assist, along with one of the student trainers. Coach Bryant yelled to Smokey to send LeBoeuf into the game. Gordon LeBoeuf was another talented player from Port Neches who was the first substitute for Gay.

Smokey yelled back to Bryant, "LeBoeuf can't come in. He's dead," which was what was said when a player was wearing a red shoelace across the shoulder pads to symbolize he was ineligible to return to the field during the current quarter. (LeBoeuf had already played in the third quarter.) Without missing a beat, Smokey then draped an arm over Gay's shoulder and said, "Son, you're not hurt as bad as you think you are, so get back in there!" The record will show that Coach Bryant, late in his career, was asked who was the toughest player he ever coached. His answer was "Richard Gay."

These are but three stories worth sharing about Smokey Harper, as seen through the eyes of one of the finest writers to ever come out of the state of Texas. Herskowitz has authored more than fifty books, including volumes about Coach Paul Bryant, John Connally, Nolan Ryan, and Gene Autry, to name but a few. Herskowitz reminded me, "Smokey had a way of telling it exactly the way he saw it." He was truly a special man and came along at a special time in Texas A&M history.

Smokey, in particular, loved the beautiful trees on the Texas A&M campus and, as the story goes, in the springtime after that first difficult season, he was walking back to Kyle Field with a couple of the assistant coaches when he heard the sound of a chain saw and recoiled at the sight of a crew cutting down one of the big oak trees. That really distressed him, and he then said to the coaches, "You know, those trees are one of the only good things about this miserable place, and here they are cutting one of them down!"

Those who came to know Smokey Harper loved and admired him. Those who didn't know him truly missed a wonderful life experience, as Mickey Herskowitz can attest.

Chapter 18

"I Like Little People!"

As the 1953 high school football season was ending in New Mexico, it was generally realized that the top running back in the state was Roswell's Loyd Taylor. During his days as a high school gridder, he forged a splendid record as a halfback. He knew how to play the game, and he also knew how to win.

He was heavily recruited by the usual cast of schools in the Southwest Conference, and Ed Price, who was then head football coach at the University of Texas, was probably the most persistent. He envisioned Taylor would fit right in as a Longhorn halfback. He could play right alongside Walter Fondren, an All-American halfback out of Houston's Lamar High School.

The problem was, Taylor already made a college choice. I learned, the last time I saw Taylor at a teammate's funeral we both attended, that there were family connections at the University of Kentucky, and Coach Paul Bryant was now preparing to welcome Taylor to the Wildcat team. Taylor's decision to be a Kentucky Wildcat was determined very early in the recruiting season.

Throughout the process, Taylor was concerned that his size would probably be a big problem for most college football head coaches. Soaking wet, Taylor weighed only 142 pounds. However, Price—who coached the New Mexico high school team in the annual All-Star game—was eager to overlook that problem inasmuch as Taylor had scored the first two touchdowns in that game. He ran for 135 yards that day.

Meanwhile, things were happening in Lexington, Kentucky. Taylor recalled receiving a phone call early in 1954 from Coach Bryant telling him he was still wanted and needed, but in College Station, Texas, and not Lexington. Taylor had already bought in to Coach Bryant, but he felt obligated to remind Coach Bryant about his weight—better yet, his lack of weight.

Coach Bryant's response was "That's fine with me. I love little people."

History will show Loyd Taylor was a complement to the backfield that included, at various times, Jack Pardee and John David Crow. Taylor was an All-SWC First Team selection, too. He was also a superb place-kicker and had excellent range for field goals. In those days, when two-way football was the way the game was played, the responsibility for kicking field goals came down to whoever in the backfield could do it best. That was, almost always, Loyd Taylor.

He was small, fast, and very shifty. He also proved to be an excellent defensive back. He loved to hit. And he was smart, too.

Following his playing career, he coached and indicated he felt quite honored to have been a member of Coach Gene Stallings's coaching staff when the 1967 Cotton Bowl found the Texas Aggies beating Coach Paul Bryant's Crimson Tide. It was a once-in-a-lifetime experience to have been in the locker room after the game when Coach Bryant came in and visited with each and every member of that team. Bryant was proud of both Gene Stallings and Loyd Taylor on the special Cotton Bowl victory day for Texas A&M

Loyd Taylor was later inducted into the Texas A&M Athletic Hall of Fame and served with distinction as the executive director of the Lettermen's Association at Texas A&M.

The Texas Aggies, Southwest Conference champions, in their locker room at Memorial Stadium in Austin, November 1956. Smokey Harper is in the front row, second from left. Author's personal collection.

Jack Pardee, 1954, sporting his new wardrobe. Courtesy Yearbook Collection, Cushing Memorial Library & Archives, Texas A&M University.

A sketch from the famous Jim Earle, commenting on the Aggies' conquest of the "Memorial Stadium jinx" and their 1956 SWC championship. Courtesy Yearbook Collection, Cushing Memorial Library & Archives, Texas A&M University.

Coach Bryant, 1957. He really didn't like being called "Bear." Courtesy Yearbook Collection, Cushing Memorial Library & Archives, Texas A&M University.

Team photo of the 1956 conference champions. Notice the handsome, slender young fellow on the left in the student manager jersey—yours truly. Courtesy Yearbook Collection, Cushing Memorial Library & Archives, Texas A&M University.

Jim Earle commemorates "the day the rains came down"—when A&M beat both TCU and the weather in 1956. Courtesy Yearbook Collection, Cushing Memorial Library & Archives, Texas A&M University.

A fitting tribute to a favorite son of Christoval, Texas: John Perry "Jack" Pardee. Courtesy Christoval Independent School District.

Jimmy Wright, from Edinburg, Texas, one helluva quarterback! Courtesy Yearbook Collection, Cushing Memorial Library & Archives, Texas A&M University.

Gary Rollins, sergebutt manager, Kyle Field, 1956. From *Then and Now: The Fiftieth Reunion of the Class of '58*, p. 74.

Before Fosbury flopped, Fritzie flew. Fritzie Connally at the Southwest Conference track and field finals, 1957. From *Then and Now: The Fiftieth Reunion of the Class of '58*, p. 73.

Here's the patch we all wore so proudly. A little tattered and worn, perhaps, but aren't we all? From *Then and Now: The Fiftieth Reunion of the Class of '58*, p. 109.

Five fabulous yell leaders, 1956–57: Jerry "Magoo" McGown, Dick Mernard, Bill Dorsey, Don Houston, and Ted Lowe, Miss Rev's favorite pooper-scooper. Courtesy Yearbook Collection, Cushing Memorial Library & Archives, Texas A&M University.

This prime-seating ticket for the 1957 A&M–Rice game went for $3.50; the ticket for the 1957 Gator Bowl matchup between A&M and Tennessee fetched the princely sum of $6.00. Trans-Texas Airways? It's long gone. From *Then and Now: The Fiftieth Reunion of the Class of '58*, p. 52.

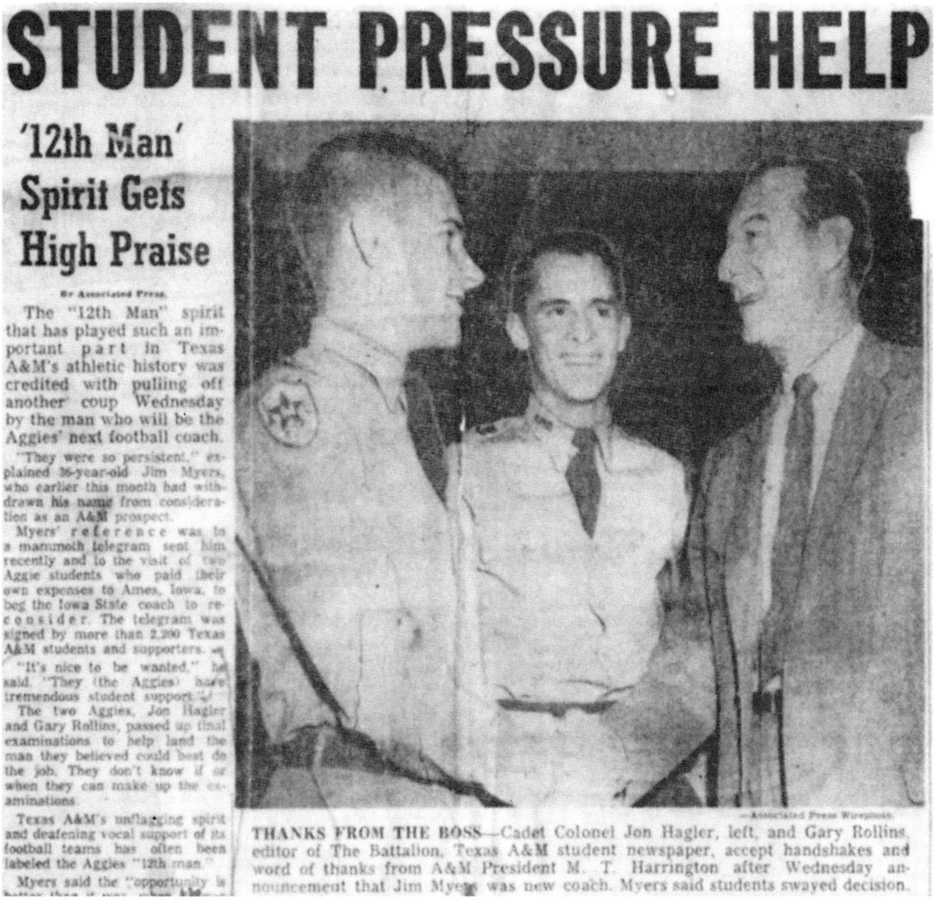

STUDENT PRESSURE HELP

'12th Man' Spirit Gets High Praise

By Associated Press.

The "12th Man" spirit that has played such an important part in Texas A&M's athletic history was credited with pulling off another coup Wednesday by the man who will be the Aggies' next football coach.

"They were so persistent," explained 36-year-old Jim Myers, who earlier this month had withdrawn his name from consideration as an A&M prospect.

Myers' reference was to a mammoth telegram sent him recently and to the visit of two Aggie students who paid their own expenses to Ames, Iowa, to beg the Iowa State coach to reconsider. The telegram was signed by more than 2,200 Texas A&M students and supporters.

"It's nice to be wanted," he said. "They (the Aggies) have tremendous student support."

The two Aggies, Jon Hagler and Gary Rollins, passed up final examinations to help land the man they believed could best do the job. They don't know if or when they can make up the examinations.

Texas A&M's unflagging spirit and deafening vocal support of its football teams has often been labeled the Aggies "12th man."

Myers said the "opportunity is

—Associated Press Wirephoto.

THANKS FROM THE BOSS—Cadet Colonel Jon Hagler, left, and Gary Rollins, editor of The Battalion, Texas A&M student newspaper, accept handshakes and word of thanks from A&M President M. T. Harrington after Wednesday announcement that Jim Myers was new coach. Myers said students swayed decision.

How in the world did two Aggies survive skipping finals for a coach recruitment trip? It helped that we sent Iowa State's Jim Meyers an 88-foot-long telegram, signed by almost the entire Corps of Cadets. The ploy worked. From ***Then and Now*: *The Fiftieth Reunion of the Class of '58***, p. 79.

Three hard-working student trainers in 1957: (*left to right*) Jerry "Rat" Rhea, Carl Gene Merrell, and Ray "Grubworm" Stevens. Courtesy Yearbook Collection, Cushing Memorial Library & Archives, Texas A&M University.

Murry Trimble was an All–Southwest Conference guard and wreaked damage with only one hand. His teammates called him "Stubby," and he marched to the beat of his own drum. Courtesy Yearbook Collection, Cushing Memorial Library & Archives, Texas A&M University.

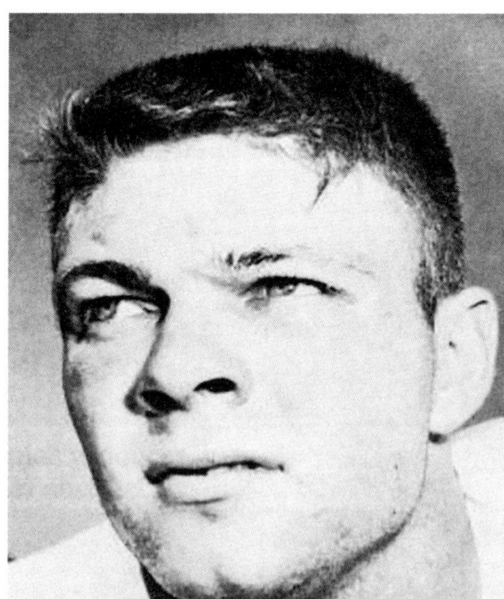

Who first called No. 44 "John David Crow"? Answer: Coach Paul Bryant. Crow once said, "If it hadn't been for Coach Bryant, folks would probably have known me as John or J. D." Courtesy Texas A&M University Athletics.

The road near Kyle Field that leads to a Heisman Trophy winner. From *Then and Now: The Fiftieth Reunion of the Class of '58*, p. 43.

The distinguished Jon Hagler, skipping finals? Not a chance! From *Then and Now: The Fiftieth Reunion of the Class of '58*, p. 39.

Red Grange, "the Galloping Ghost" (kneeling with football), and nationally known broadcaster Lindsey Nelson dropped by practice to offer some pointers to Coach Bryant's starters. From *Then and Now: The Fiftieth Reunion of the Class of '58*, p. 58.

Roddy Osborne scores against the teasips behind Jack Pardee's block. Osborne was a tough, talented, versatile player who loved to hit. Every so often, he might attempt a pass. Courtesy Yearbook Collection, Cushing Memorial Library & Archives, Texas A&M University.

John David Crow makes sure reporter Mickey Herskowitz spells his name correctly. From *Then and Now: The Fiftieth Reunion of the Class of '58*, p. 69.

Charles "Smokey" Harper: war hero, pioneer athletic trainer, and outstanding mentor to athletes, student trainers, and others. Author's personal collection.

The "hurricane game" with TCU was a big, big day for No. 84. TCU was probably asking, "Who is this guy?" Appelt, not Crow, was famous for a day. From ***Then and Now*: *The Fiftieth Reunion of the Class of '58***, p. 71.

Jack Powell, Jack Pardee, and John David Crow oversee Gene "Bebes" Stallings and Lloyd Hale during practice. Courtesy Texas A&M University Athletics.

Little did we all know that Coach Zapalac had been voted Best Blocker for the 1938 Texas A&M national championship team. Back in the day, he was known as "Wild Willie." From *Then and Now: The Fiftieth Reunion of the Class of '58*, p. 55.

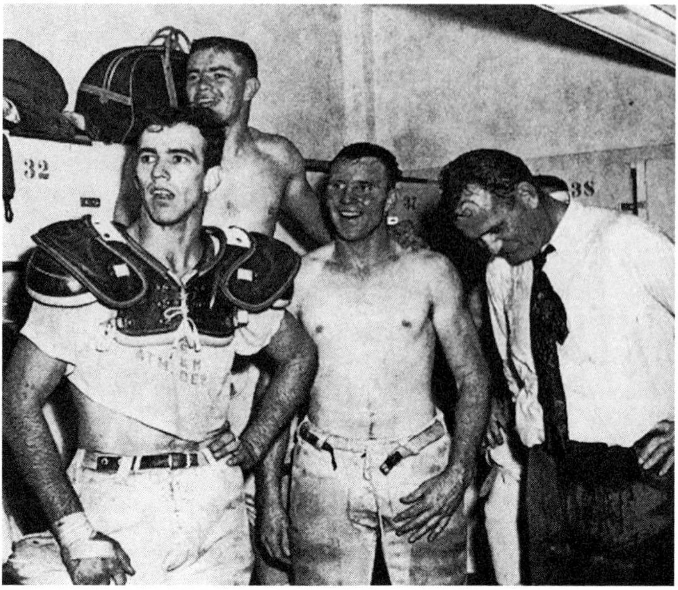

Left to right: Bobby Lockett, Lloyd Hale, and Jack Pardee celebrate a long-awaited victory with a wet and happy Coach Bryant. Memorial Stadium, November 1956. Author's personal collection.

Roddy Osborne passed, and Bobby Joe Conrad came down with the reception to set up an Aggie touchdown against LSU, 1956. Courtesy Yearbook Collection, Cushing Memorial Library & Archives, Texas A&M University.

One of the finest coaching staffs ever assembled. Most went on to head coaching jobs, where their success continued. From the Rice vs. Texas A&M game program, 1954. Author's personal collection.

Buddy Payne was an excellent player, but who would have forecast that he would later become president of the 12th Man Foundation and the Letterman's Association? Courtesy Yearbook Collection, Cushing Memorial Library & Archives, Texas A&M University.

Cadet Jon Hagler '58, who skipped finals to help recruit Jim Meyers at Iowa State for A&M's head football coach. How about that for Aggie spirit? From *Then and Now: The Fiftieth Reunion of the Class of '58*, p. 37.

Dennis Goehring, a "too-small" Junction Boy who was selected as an All–Southwest Conference guard. Courtesy Yearbook Collection, Cushing Memorial Library & Archives, Texas A&M University.

Allen was Dennis Goehring's younger brother, also smallish, but tough and ornery. He lost his life by heroically flying his jet fighter into a mountainside in Japan rather than risk crashing in a heavily populated area. Courtesy Yearbook Collection, Cushing Memorial Library & Archives, Texas A&M University.

Dr. Richard Steadman left Texas A&M to attend medical school and later became recognized as one of the most influential orthopedic surgeons in the world. Courtesy Yearbook Collection, Cushing Memorial Library & Archives, Texas A&M University.

Bobby Nichols came to Texas A&M to play football, but he became famous as the first Aggie to win the PGA championship. Coach Bryant frequently partnered with him in golf tournaments. Talk about a ringer! Courtesy Yearbook Collection, Cushing Memorial Library & Archives, Texas A&M University.

Every Saturday thousands of Texans followed Southwest Conference football on the radio, listening to the Humble Network broadcasts. From the Rice vs. Texas A&M game program, 1954. Author's personal collection.

Loyd Taylor barely weighed 140 pounds when Coach Bryant recruited him, but the coach told him, "I like little people." Courtesy Yearbook Collection, Cushing Memorial Library & Archives, Texas A&M University.

John Gilbert anchored the Aggie line at center. Gilbert, like Coach Bryant, called Arkansas home. Courtesy Texas A&M University Athletics.

Gordon LeBoeuf was a rough, tough fullback and linebacker from the Golden Triangle. Courtesy Yearbook Collection, Cushing Memorial Library & Archives, Texas A&M University.

Don Watson was a swift, shifty guy who earned the nickname "Frog Killer." Courtesy Yearbook Collection, Cushing Memorial Library & Archives, Texas A&M University.

"Bonnie Prince Charlie" Milstead was a terrific passer, an overall outstanding quarterback, and a scholar—a winner in every way. Courtesy Yearbook Collection, Cushing Memorial Library & Archives, Texas A&M University.

Charlie Krueger from Caldwell, Texas, was an All–Southwest Conference performer and an All-American tackle who spent many years excelling in the NFL. Courtesy Yearbook Collection, Cushing Memorial Library & Archives, Texas A&M University.

Gene "Bebes" Stallings, one of Coach Bryant's Junction Boys, weighed 180 pounds when the Aggies played the Rice Owls in 1954. His Aggie team beat Bryant's Crimson Tide in the 1968 Cotton Bowl. He later won a national championship as head coach at Alabama. A classy guy, a class act, and a superb Texas Aggie. Courtesy Yearbook Collection, Cushing Memorial Library & Archives, Texas A&M University; and author's personal collection.

Billy Pete Huddleston, history will show, was one of the most successful and most gifted Texas Aggies of all time. He was a generous guy, a brilliant businessman, and simply represented the very best example of what a Junction Boy should ultimately become by none other than Coach Paul "Bear" Bryant. Cushing Memorial Library & Archives, Texas A&M University.

Chapter 19

Dr. Richard Steadman, Left Tackle

Dick Steadman was not your average high school student. In fact, he was way, way above average. And as his days in high school were nearing an end in the spring of 1955 in Fairborn, Ohio, he had already been accepted to attend Harvard when he received a long-distance phone call from Coach Paul Bryant in College Station, Texas.

You see, Steadman—in addition to excelling as an exceptional student academically—was also a pretty darned good tackle on both offense and defense. That automatically made him Coach Bryant's kind of a guy: an All-Star on the field and an All-Star in class.

Coach Bryant's reaching out to him at his family residence in Ohio proved to be both timely and meaningful. Even though Steadman was born in Sherman, Texas, his father was in the military and this meant he and his family lived in many different places during the course of his father's career. Steadman shelved his plans to enroll at Harvard and accepted Coach Bryant's offer to come to Texas A&M as a member of the Class of '59's crop of signees. Steadman was in good company as he logged in alongside recent Aggie newcomers like Charlie Milstead, Allen Goehring, Luther Hall, and Byron Carruthers.

There was no question about it. There were plenty of tough practices ahead on the near horizon. There was a problem, however. Steadman had expressed his long-range goal to become a physician when Coach Bryant first approached him about a football scholarship. And so Coach Bryant knew about his ambition and most certainly realized Steadman had the qualifications to reach his ultimate goal.

The record shows that Dick Steadman was a member of two of Coach Bryant's teams in 1956 and 1957. But in the middle of his second season, he came to realize the pressures of performing both on the field and in the classroom were becoming too great for him to overcome or even endure. Accordingly, he sat down with Coach Bryant and simply shared the fact that the combination of long, difficult practices followed by position meetings usually meant unreasonably long nights studying just to stay on course for admission to medical school.

It was Steadman's belief that attaining a high level of academic accomplishment was critical if he was to be accepted into medical school. And adhering to the demands of football practice and all that entailed was suddenly in direct conflict with his plans for a future in medicine.

To his surprise, Coach Bryant responded in a positive manner. Steadman valued his athletic scholarship and enjoyed playing football, but his career target was to become a physician. Coach Bryant then said Steadman's participation in team workouts would be at his discretion. In other words, academics trumped football. He was assured that his standing as a team member would not be blemished. Basically, he was given permission to skip practice in light of a larger goal in his life. Each day, his locker contained his football gear, but no mention was ever made about the special understanding between Steadman and Coach Bryant. He practiced when he could and that was that. He received special tutoring in the finer art of playing both offensive and defensive tackle by none other than Charlie Krueger.

Near the end of the second year, Steadman received word that his application for medical school at the University of Texas Southwestern Medical School in Dallas had been approved, and he was eager to share the news with Coach Bryant. He recently recalled that Coach Bryant couldn't have been nicer about learning his good news. He draped that big arm of friendship across Steadman's shoulder and wished him the very best in his medical career.

Little did Coach Bryant know that this talented young football player was destined to become one of the most famous orthopedic surgeons in the world. Let me amend that statement. Dr. Richard Steadman became known worldwide as the *best* orthopedic surgeon in the world. Here's why that reputation is well founded.

A renowned innovator and mentor in the field of orthopedic sports medicine, Dr. Steadman is internationally known for the development of several advanced surgical procedures for the knee, including the "healing response," and, in 2011, the "package," a technique that can restore normal comfortable movement to the stiff and painful arthritic knee.

He has treated numerous professional athletes across various sports and is sought out by some of the world's best-known athletes and public figures for treatment. His ability to return high-level athletes with knee injuries to medal-winning victories following surgery and rehab with him has made him an iconic figure in sports medicine. Traumatic knee injuries occur in multiple sports, and Dr. Steadman's success in returning many elite athletes to major achievements following potentially career-ending injuries include twenty-six athletes from professional soccer, forty-five from the NFL, twenty-three from MLB, eight in the NBA, and twenty-six snow skiers.

Dr. Steadman has been a consultant to the Denver Broncos football team and the Colorado Rockies baseball team and has served as US Alpine Team physician for the following Winter Olympics:

1976 Innsbruck, Austria
1980 Lake Placid, USA
1984 Sarajevo, Bosnia-Herzegovina (formerly Yugoslavia)
1988 Calgary, Canada
1992 Albertville, France
1994 Lillehammer, Norway
1998 Nagano, Japan
2002 Salt Lake City, USA
2006 Torino, Italy

Some of his specialties include:

Arthroscopic knee surgery
Open knee surgery
Osteoarthritis of the knee
Joint restoration and preservation techniques
ACL knee injuries
MCL knee injuries
Knee instability
Knee pain
Patellofemoral pain syndrome
Chondral defects of the knee

And finally, Dr. Steadman's list of honors, awards, and accomplishments would require an additional page—single-spaced.

A final story is worth sharing. Rat Rhea was serving as head athletic trainer for the Atlanta Falcons a few years ago, and he recently shared this recollection from his days in Atlanta:

> I began reading various medical presentations in orthopedic journals by a Richard Steadman, M.D. Most of these presentations dealt with injuries to highly competitive athletes from various sports. Winter sports seemed to dominate his presentations; many dealing with Olympic athletes from all nations.
>
> Our Falcons team orthopedist had attended a mid-winter meeting in Colorado. This group was called the Rocky Mountain Traumatology Society. He would come back each year and tell of what new things they discussed and how they might pertain to the Atlanta Falcons. One year, he came back and told me that he had been visiting with Dick Steadman and Dick told him that he had been a football player at Texas A&M. Only then did I realize that this was *our* Dick Steadman. I had been reading presentations from an internationally acclaimed sports medicine orthopedist for years and had never realized this was the same Dick Steadman we knew back in the Bryant era in Aggieland.
>
> Turning the clock back to my days when I was a senior student trainer at Texas A&M, I did recall Dick Steadman had left the squad to enter medical school. It was many years later I successfully connected the dots. That Dr. Dick Steadman was our Dick Steadman!

Indeed, it was!

Dr. Steadman is now retired but spends most of the year in Vail, Colorado. When not in Vail, he and his wife, Gay, enjoy life in California's San Juan Capistrano. When asked what was the most valuable lesson he learned while at Texas A&M, he confessed it was "not to line up against Charlie Krueger."

Chapter 20

Those Hallettsville Boys

Bill Appelt and George Gillar were two good old country boys who grew up together in Hallettsville. They first played football together in high school when Gillar was a junior and Appelt was a sophomore. That also happened to be when they first met at the very first football game each one of them ever saw.

Their head football coach was Emmet Clark, a tough former marine and grizzled veteran who had fought in North Korea. He was a no-nonsense, take-no-prisoners coach and a lot like Coach Paul Bryant. He ran a tight ship: no swearing, no carbonated drinks, and probably no girls.

If you were injured, you played unless a bone wasn't sticking out somewhere. That, too, later reminded Appelt of Smokey Harper at Texas A&M. The only answers Coach Clark accepted were "Yes, sir" and "No, sir."

As was the case in most Texas towns during the fall, high school football in Hallettsville was the only game in town. Just for fun, Hallettsville was once cited in *Ripley's Believe It or Not* as the "13 City" because, in 1913, it had thirteen letters in the name, a population of 1,300, thirteen churches, thirteen newspapers, and even thirteen saloons.

On the practice field one day, Appelt recalled that he once stumbled back to the huddle after a big hit and Coach Clark, after a quick assessment of his bloodied nose and the overall medical situation, simply said, "You'll be all right. Just get back in there."

Appelt, a junior, had played some football but Gillar had no experience. Appelt was an end and Gillar a halfback. Gillar was slue-footed, as well, but that didn't hamper his ability to run. He was fast! But when he ran in track meets, he tended to flail all over the place and knock the other runners out of their lanes.

Appelt recalled there were no set plays. He would simply tell Gillar to run over their right tackle or take a pitch and run around left end. If there happened to be a brick wall nearby, Gillar would have tried to punch a hole in it. He was that kind of a guy. Frank Sinatra would have loved him.

One day in fall practice, as Appelt was running "go routes," he became aware that guys were frantically yelling at him as he ran full speed down the sideline. The quarterback's long pass arrived at the exact moment Appelt slammed head first into a light pole at the side of the practice field.

Everyone rushed over to see if he was okay. Appelt was laid out flat, with creosote tar on both his face and jersey. Coach Clark, the first to arrive, calmly said, "Just lie here a while. You'll be okay." And then he looked down at Appelt and growled, "You know you're not hurt so bad that you can't play tomorrow night."

The *Hallettsville Herald-Tribune*, the local newspaper, offered free tickets to the movie for players who made "big plays." Appelt won tickets that week for running into a light pole. It must have been a slow news week.

After graduation, both of those guys enrolled at Victoria Junior College, where they played football and ran track together. Gillar's track coach fixed his awkward gait and he improved his 100-yard dash time from 10.5 to 9.8. It was while they were running track in high school that they first met and competed against Sugar Land's Kenneth Hall, who became their teammate at A&M.

Appelt's Victoria JC coach was Rusty Russell, who had previously coached at SMU. He asked Appelt if he was interested in playing more football after junior college. Appelt indicated he thought he'd like to attend TCU in Fort Worth, but Russell said that was not the school for Appelt because it offered no agricultural courses. Also, Russell didn't think Appelt would fit into Abe Martin's scheme.

The only place for Appelt—and Gillar—was Texas A&M, where the two could play for Coach Paul Bryant. And be farmers, to boot. Coach Bryant had been invited to be a guest speaker at the school's football banquet; while he was there, Russell approached him and nominated Appelt for Bryant's consideration.

His pitch went like this: "Bill's not real big. He's not really what you would call fast. He can't catch every pass. He runs decent routes. And he loves to hit."

Coach Bryant said, "Son, we don't care about your size or your speed one bit. If you like to hit and you have a good attitude, you can play for me."

It was close to a package deal with Gillar. He was not that big, but he was definitely fast and he didn't know the meaning of the word "quit." "If his guts were hanging out, he would still want to run the next play," Appelt said.

And so Coach Bryant left Victoria and promised that the SWC letter of intent would either be delivered by Coach Willie Zapalac or mailed to the two young men. Either way, both were headed to Aggieland. While on campus, they roomed together. They were about the same size. If one of them bought a new shirt, they would take turns wearing it. They owned one tie between them.

At fall practice, later on, Gillar found himself at the bottom of a pile of players after a play, and everyone was shocked to see a serious gash in his calf. Players wore screw-on cleats, and someone's cleat post had caused a hideous gash on Gillar's calf. Smokey thought it might be best to take him inside where he could be stitched up. Gillar, on the other hand, wanted to keep playing.

It was at that moment that Coach Bryant loudly proclaimed, "I wish we had some more guys like this who don't know how to quit."

Which brings us back to Coach Zapalac. Appelt related there was an issue with the pronunciation of his position coach's name. Most everyone called him "Coach Zap-a-lack," but Appelt unwittingly made the apparent error of pronouncing his name as it would have been said in and around Bellville, Coach Z's hometown. In Bellville it was pronounced "Zap-a-losh." Appelt recalled that he once addressed his position coach as "Coach Zap-a-losh" and could tell, pretty darned quick, that Coach Zapalac didn't like having his named pronounced that way.

Shortly thereafter, Coach Zapalac directed Appelt to get into a blocking stance and be prepared to learn how Coach Zapalac wanted him to block. The forearm the coach delivered clearly indicated he did not want to be called Coach Zap-a-losh ever again.

Appelt and Gillar were both Texas A&M lettermen and major contributors on the field for the Texas Aggies championship team. These days, Appelt and his wife, Jean, enjoy a quiet retired life back in his old hometown of Hallettsville. His high school pal, George Gillar, passed away a few years ago but is still fondly remembered. He ended up as a land and apartment baron, surprising everyone who never realized he had that kind of capability.

If you happen to be in Hallettsville, Appelt will be happy to show you that certificate he earned for the movie tickets. And he will also show you the hometown newspaper story that ran the week after he personally "won" the Texas A&M–TCU game—or at least his jersey did. It's hilarious!

Chapter 21

Bonnie Prince Charlie

Charlie Milstead was a super-talented high school All-American quarterback out of Tyler's John Tyler High School who set all sorts of passing records. He came to Texas A&M because he wanted to play for Coach Paul Bryant. And Coach Bryant wanted Charlie, too.

The problem was, there was one other high school quarterback in Texas that Coach Bryant also wanted as badly as he wanted Milstead. His name was Don Meredith, and he had the same kind of astonishing passing records. He also played basketball. Some said he was an even better basketball player than he was a quarterback.

Coach Bryant requested an opportunity to meet with Charlie Milstead and his family and came to Tyler in the spring of 1956 to spell out where and how Milstead would fit into the Aggies' rapidly emerging program. It is no secret that Coach Bryant placed a high value on establishing a strong relationship with each player's mother, and this trip was no exception.

When I visited with Milstead and his family not that long ago, Milstead mentioned one fact that stood out—quite vividly—in his late mother's recollection of that day when the family met with Coach Bryant. Each and every time Mrs. Milstead entered the room, Coach Bryant would stand up. It was a respectful gesture, and Mrs. Milstead appreciated and long remembered his courtesy. She endorsed young Milstead's acceptance of an offer to attend Texas A&M. And Coach Bryant pleased one and all when he agreed to also offer a scholarship to Byron Carruthers, Tyler's exceptional receiver and Milstead's favorite target. Carruthers, by the way, rose to a prominent role managing Six Flags Over Texas as his career moved along at a rapid pace.

Mrs. Milstead also asked Coach Bryant to promise he would not leave Texas A&M while her son was still enrolled at Texas A&M. Coach Bryant gave her his promise.

Thus, when he made his decision to leave A&M and return to Alabama, Mrs. Milstead was deeply disappointed. Bryant, it was reported, offered Milstead an opportunity to transfer to Alabama, but it was simply too late. And not enough.

But back to Meredith for a moment. Don Meredith really, really wanted to play for Coach Bryant. But the thought of playing at Texas A&M—no girls, no bright lights, no big-city atmosphere for a guy who would soon thereafter be dubbed "Dandy Don"—made it a tough pill to swallow. He really, really wanted to play for Coach Bryant, but he also really, really could not fathom playing at a place still called "Sing-Sing on the Brazos."

So he became a Mustang. He just couldn't pull the trigger on Coach Bryant's offer to become a Texas Aggie. And what an unbelievable career he enjoyed, both at SMU and in the NFL. It seems also relevant to mention the many years he performed brilliantly as an NFL television announcer alongside Frank Gifford and Howard Cosell. One could only imagine what might have ultimately transpired if each of these two talented quarterbacks had flipped schools: Meredith as a Texas Aggie, Milstead as an SMU Mustang.

Here's an interesting memory. During the 1957 season Meredith entered the game against the Aggies in the third quarter of a game on Kyle Field as quarterback. The Aggies were SWC Conference champions from the previous season, of course. It was during this game that SMU opened the third quarter by dropping back into what was then called a "short punt" formation. Now they call it the shotgun. The formation was a new weapon for SMU, and the Mustangs thought it might catch the A&M team unprepared.

The Aggies' defense had been coached to be both prepared and aggressive if and when the other team suddenly sprang into a surprise formation. As Meredith prepared to receive the snap, the Aggie defense shifted into a Gap 8 alignment—our goal line defense, simply stated—and when the ball was snapped, two or three Aggies arrived about the same time. Second and third downs? Same result. They punted on fourth-and-a-mile. That was the end of that formation for the game.

One other memory is worthy of mentioning. In one of Milstead's early appearances as the A&M quarterback, as he approached the line of scrimmage, he noted that the defensive backs—the corner backs, primarily—were leaving the wide receivers uncovered.

So he hand-signaled the receivers and, after the ball was snapped, flipped a no-sweat touchdown pass to one of the wideouts. It was a proud moment for Milstead.

But as he returned to the bench, Coach Bryant seized him by the shoulder pads and got up close to his face and said, "Don't you ever do that again! We don't want them to think this is too easy for us. You call the plays we agreed on or you won't play for me!"

After Coach Bryant left for Tuscaloosa, Milstead found himself playing quarterback for Coach Jim Myers, who replaced Coach Bryant. Myers's teams ran the single wing—not the best formation for a passing quarterback—but Milstead still was a consensus SWC selection in 1958. What made Mrs. Milstead beam, however, was her son's selection to the Academic All-America team in 1959.

Milstead played twenty-two games in his professional career. He was originally drafted in the fourteenth round by the Washington Redskins. He spent minimal time as a quarterback but excelled both as a punter and a defensive back. He spent his two final years with the Houston Oilers, the AFL's two-time champion.

There is a separate and even more impressive story about this fine Texas Aggie. He and five of his teammates ultimately spent their entire careers working together and enjoying business success at a level they could never have anticipated. It all goes back to those hot, dusty afternoons on the practice field behind Kyle Field when they learned how to compete and win.

Charlie Milstead, who now lives in quiet retirement with his lovely wife in Houston, can now enjoy watching his children and grandchildren follow the path he formed for all of them. That's how Prince Charlie became a king! But there is more to this story, so listen up.

One day prior to practice, Ray Stevens recalled Smokey taping the ankles of one of the linemen—a junior—and asking if he had formed any opinions about the new crop of freshmen from the Class of '60. In Smokey's lingo, he wanted to know if any of those new kids was really "wuffashit." The letterman lineman said, "Smokey, I cannot answer that one. Who knows? These young kids are just like I was when I first came to Kyle Field. They are nervous and scared and they're lining up against some really good football players."

He then said, "I'll tell you what. Let's look at these guys ten or twenty years after they leave A&M and then we can make a decision as to whether or not they were wuffashit."

Charlie Milstead and Joe Schmid formed a special bond. Schmid was next in line after I moved on to *The Battalion*, and he frequently sold players' game tickets and shared the proceeds. Milstead was impressed with Schmid and his integrity. Schmid was an engineer and, like your author, a Houston/San Jacinto graduate who wanted to go into business in his own hometown after he graduated.

Schmid went to work in Houston for Doug Toole & Company and stayed in close touch with Milstead. After college, Milstead was drafted by both the NFL's Washington Redskins and the AFL's San Diego Chargers. Schmid had contacts in Houston and theorized that things might work out better for Milstead if he could play in Houston. The Chargers made a deal that sent Milstead to Houston.

There is a cute story about Milstead's signing bonus. Milstead met with Bud Adams, the gregarious owner of the Oilers, and as Adams began to peel off $100 bills, he told Milstead to say "Stop!" when Milstead felt the signing offer was right. Milstead felt $1,000 was fair. It was a sweetheart deal in more ways than one.

Adams paid Milstead $18,000 a year to play for the Oilers, and Schmid arranged for Milstead to work part time for Doug Toole & Company when he wasn't playing football. He made $30,000 between the two jobs. Milstead would work only on Mondays (the Oilers' day off) and full time when not playing football.

Schmid's hiring of Milstead was a solid move. Milstead spent two seasons with the Oilers and won two championship rings. Lou Rymkus was head football coach, and he traded Milstead to the New York Jets.

The Milstead family had young son Charlie in the nest, and Mark was on the way to joining the family when Milstead made the decision to retire from football. Lyle was not yet a sparkle in his mother's eye. The family wanted no part of raising a family in New York. Houston was then and forever more home to the Milstead family.

Milstead's involvement with Doug Tool & Company blossomed, and the company became Mil-Toole & Company. In 1963 Schmid bought out Toole, and it became Environmental Improvements in 1966. That's what it is today.

Schmid and Milstead had a partner in Austin named Mike Fuller. The company ultimately sold to the current ownership in 2004. They are a rep firm in the water and waste management business and represent fifty companies. Lyle Milstead, the youngest Milstead, now has Bucky Richardson as his business partner. Larry Kelm, another Aggie footballer, was a part of the business but passed away not that many years ago.

Because of the lineage dating back to the days on Kyle Field at Texas A&M, Schmid and Milstead frequently paired up with Howard "Buddy" Payne, a Houston fellow who went to Austin High School prior to coming to Aggieland. Buddy Payne was also in the rep business and worked in the electrical supply business. The Milsteads worked with municipalities and utility companies. There was much crossover business that yielded great results for both organizations.

There is a separate story in this book that profiles the almost unbelievable job Buddy Payne did both with his business and with his numerous activities on behalf of Texas A&M. Payne passed away late in 2018, and his life was celebrated at Memorial Drive United Methodist Church when more than a thousand friends, relatives, and Texas A&M teammates showed up to share their love and memories.

Smokey Harper would have been so very proud of Milstead, Schmid, Gale Oliver, Payne, Jim Harrison, and Joe Musgrove, all teammates of that Class of '60, which forged an unbelievable record of accomplishment both on the gridiron and in the business world. In retrospect, you would have to admit both Milstead and Payne were princes who rose to be recognized as kings for so many good reasons.

Chapter 22

Dub Kendrick from Cowtown

Not every high schooler recruited by the Texas Aggies in the spring of 1954 was a big, old farm boy. There were some of the new guys who were simply targeting Texas A&M from their earliest days.

Dub Kendrick, a member of the Class of '58, was one of those fellows. He called Fort Worth his home and attended Arlington Heights High School. The Yellow Jackets were, traditionally, a highly regarded team that was typically ranked in Texas' Top Ten. Kendrick's first baby picture featured him wearing a maroon and white helmet. And from that point on, he bled maroon and prayed there would come a day when he could be a Texas Aggie and play football for the Aggies on Kyle Field.

Kendrick was genuinely excited when Coach Bryant was hired and even more elated because his uncle, Marion Pugh, was solidly in his corner. Pugh, a proud member of the Texas A&M Class of '39, was quarterback on the 1939 Texas Aggies' championship football team. He also lettered as an Aggie baseball player and, in later years, owned Pugh Hardware, a thriving lumber and hardware company serving the Bryan–College Station community.

Kendrick was an end. He stood six feet four and weighed 200 pounds. And he was fast. Back in the early 1950s, that was considered darned good size for a high schooler. Unfortunately, in the spring of his senior year, he blew out his left knee and was forced to rehab it while wondering if that injury might end up disqualifying him from consideration at Texas A&M.

As his knee gradually healed, he resumed his track workouts and caught the attention of Jerry Claiborne, the Aggies' assistant coach, who recruited North Texas and who would one day become his position coach. While competing in the low hurdles event at his district track meet, Claiborne witnessed Kendrick finishing second—no small feat for a start he described as his worst ever.

Claiborne's supportive vote back in Aggieland apparently counted because, a short time later, Uncle Marion called Kendrick with the news that Texas A&M had offered him a provisional football scholarship. Basically, it was contingent on his making the team while also affording him the opportunity to overcome his knee problems. He went from deep despair to enthusiastic exultation upon hearing the good news from Uncle Marion.

When Kendrick arrived at the early preseason fish workouts, he realized he had his work cut out for him. The incoming class of players was both deep and talented. As an end, he realized he should feel fortunate to be running on the third team. The first and second teams featured players who were All-State performers in both Texas and Louisiana. There were seven freshmen teams in all, so a third team ranking was not that discouraging, all things considered.

Nonetheless, he participated as best he could in the early practices. At that time, the coaching staff would typically post the day's practice schedule consisting of a player's team ranking along with a color. All of the squad wore white practice jerseys, and slip-on colored vests were used to identify team ranking. Red, blue, and green were typically first-, second-, and third-teamers.

On this particular day, instead of reporting to the fish practice area, the first three teams were told to report to the varsity field. The previous weekend, the varsity had absorbed a painful loss on Kyle Field to the Texas Tech Red Raiders. The final score was 41-6, and the actual game wasn't even that close. The varsity team had survived ten days in Junction but found themselves sorely lacking against a talented, deep Red Raider team. The ten Aggie fumbles was but one statistic that was painful to recall.

Nonetheless, on that day, members of the fish team knew they were facing off against an older, more experienced squad of upperclassmen, so there was an element of fear present. However, Kendrick recalled his impression, as he looked down and across the line, that the fish team was bigger—and faster, it would be learned. In fact, the fish team was substantially better than the team that had been throttled by the Red Raiders from Lubbock just that past weekend.

The next day, the same fish teams were directed back to the fish field and told to sit in a wide circle. They all waited nervously for Coach Bryant to appear. And appear he did. He stepped to the center of the circle and said,

"You young men have already shown me you have what it takes to be a national champion team. You cannot be a national champion if you cannot beat a national champion team. And so, on this very day, Texas A&M has scheduled a game against the national champions." Who was that team?

Realizing Coach Bryant had nothing but admiration and respect for Gen. Bob Neyland and the Tennessee Volunteers, that was probably the team that was scheduled for a game at some point in the not-too-distant future. And Tennessee had recently nailed a national championship. Thus, a game that would take place long after Coach Bryant had left College Station and headed for Tuscaloosa was apparently scheduled.

Kendrick confessed it was one of the most powerful recollections he could recall from his days in Aggieland. Shortly thereafter, he dinged his already-damaged knee and had to sit down with Coach Bryant and confess he felt he could no longer compete. The climb uphill was simply too steep and the competition too talented.

Coach Bryant was both understanding and gracious and assured Kendrick he would be welcomed into any outfit he chose for his post-football tenure at Texas A&M. He selected Company A, Signal Corps. And he still expresses great pride in the realization that he maintains contact with both his former teammates and his fish buddies from his Signal Corps outfit.

There is something to be said for having a great Aggie uncle solidly in your corner. It was probably Uncle Marion who bought that Aggie helmet when Kendrick was still bunking in a crib. Kendrick now enjoys retired life in North Texas and still bleeds maroon every Saturday during football season.

Chapter 23

Rice vs. Texas A&M

One of the most exciting college football games ever occurred on Saturday, November 12, 1955, in Rice Stadium. I was the most senior football manager at that time and came oh-so-very-close to spending that day in jail.

You see, Coach Paul Bryant and I had a deal. He had access to eight super-prime seats at each game, and those tickets were highly sought. These days, the home team traditionally stations the visitors in a large block of seats in the corner of the end zone. But this was a time when those seats provided to Coach Bryant and his coaching staff—and players—were pretty close to the 50-yard line.

Before each game, he would hand over his eight tickers and, while the team was suiting up and participating in pregame position meetings, I'd mingle with the crowd outside the ticketing area and seek buyers. As a manager, I wore white coveralls, and I am pretty sure I sported a white Texas A&M cap with a maroon block *T*. More on that topic later.

Back then, a ticket cost $3.50, and that doesn't really sound like much, but you could then buy a gallon of gasoline for a quarter. For $3.50, you could fill your tank with some of that fine Humble Oil gasoline that Kern Tips recommended each and every Saturday during football season.

Usually, I also had a small batch of players' tickets to sell, inasmuch as each guy was provided with four seats to each game. The rules were the same, in either case. I'd sell the tickers and split the haul with either Coach Bryant or the player. Coach Bryant most assuredly knew that I, like most of the young Aggies, had zero money.

There was an element of trust involved as well. A ticket on the 50-yard line was more valuable than the face value, $3.50. But let's just say, for demonstration purposes, the asking price for a super-prime seat was $10.00. To a well-heeled person with a fat wallet, $10.00 was a deal.

And so business was brisk that day, and I realized I would soon have all of the tickets sold when I suddenly felt a firm hand on my shoulder and turned to face a Houston police officer. He told me in no uncertain terms that scalping tickets was against the law, and then he marched me straight back to the Texas A&M dressing room.

Coach Bryant happened to be near the door when the policeman walked through with his hand still on my shoulder. Looking alarmed, Coach Bryant hurried over and listened intently—with a scowl on his face—as the policeman revealed that I was blatantly breaking the law. Coach Bryant was warm in thanking the fellow for doing his job, and he promised he would see I was properly disciplined. He then called Smokey Harper, who was also standing nearby, and asked Smokey to retrieve a football. He asked the cop if he had any sons and, when he learned he did, he gave him the football and thanked him for bringing my indiscretion to his attention.

My heart was pounding as the fellow left. Coach Bryant then asked me how the ticket sales were going. I said things were going great, right up to the moment when I was placed under house arrest. At that point, Coach Bryant said, "Hustle on over to the other side of the stadium and sell the rest of those tickets. But be sure to keep an eye out for that policeman." I did what he suggested and sold all of the tickets.

Back to the game. Coach Bryant probably disliked Rice more than any of the Southwest Conference foes. You see, the tenured, esteemed Rice coach, Jess Neely, would be the driving force behind the Aggies' landing on probation in 1956. For another thing, Houston was a hotbed for football talent, and the arrival of Bryant rankled Neely. He was a good coach and an excellent recruiter, and he could usually cherry-pick the Houston football crop and offer scholarships to fellows who might even be a few brain cells short of genius level. Rice is an academically tough school and, back then, had a few majors that afforded a young man the opportunity to play football and then ease into the business world with a decent education. But Bryant's arrival in Aggieland changed the calculus for Neely's recruiting.

This was the second game a Bryant-coached team had played against the Rice Owls. In 1954 the Aggies' Junction Boys fought long and hard against Neely's guys but lost on Kyle Field, 29-19. Thus, Neely and the Owls knew this second game would be a hard-fought contest. This game featured a Texas A&M team that was young, fast, and talented. The Rice Owls were older, bigger, and almost as fast and talented. The scene was set.

The first three quarters were scoreless as both teams slugged it out, toe to toe. Early in the fourth quarter, Rice scored not once but twice. The game clock reflected that there were but four minutes and fifteen seconds left when the sizable crowd began to filter out of Rice Stadium. Up in the press box the ink-stained wretches tapped out an ending to the game story and prepared to head for the respective locker rooms.

My job as student manager included the chore of hustling back to the locker room to uncap the bottles of Coca-Cola. It was a typically steamy Houston Saturday afternoon in November, and a cold drink of Coke was then advertised as "the pause that refreshes."

Here's what happened while I was doing what I did. In the final four minutes and fifteen seconds, the Fightin' Texas Aggies scored three touchdowns and stunned everyone in the whole wide world of sports. The Aggies won 20-12.

Back in the locker room, I was aware of the increased noise level outside, but I was totally unprepared for the gleeful gang of Aggies who stormed into the locker room and began celebrating one of the biggest and most amazing victories in college football. I missed the on-field finale of that game. To this day, every guy—or maybe I should say, any of those guys who are still living in their eighties—can vividly remember that game.

With 4:15 on the clock, the Aggies had the ball on their side of the 50-yard line. Loyd Taylor, the Aggies' halfback, took a pitch and scooted downfield 52 yards to the Rice 3. Taylor then scored two plays later and kicked the extra point to cut the lead to 12-7, Owls.

Jack Powell's perfectly executed onside kick was covered by Gene Stallings at the Rice 43. This was a play that was practiced during the week over and over again. Powell would approach the ball and, instead of hitting the football dead center, would hit to the right of the center line of the ball. Thus, the ball would create a curve and actually move back on its axis toward the kicking team. Think of it as a big *C* arc. Powell hit the ball perfectly. It curved back and Stallings fell on it.

On the very first play, Jimmy Wright zipped a pass on the sideline to Taylor, who hauled it in at the Rice 5 and crossed the goal line for a touchdown. Another Taylor extra point was tacked on. In less than one minute, Taylor accounted for fourteen Aggie points. In a row.

The Owls were in full panic mode. After receiving the kickoff, it was almost "Hail, Mary" time and King Hill's downfield heave ended up in the hands of none other than Jack Pardee.

The Aggies were coached to yell "Bingo!" when an interception occurred, and that's what everyone heard as Pardee eluded tacklers downfield. He was finally hauled down at the Rice 3. Don Watson sprinted into the end zone with the final touchdown and secured a 20-12 victory over the crestfallen Rice Owls team. When the game ended, the Aggies held the ball on the Rice 4-yard line.

Rice Stadium, at that point, had probably seen the crowd diminished by one-third. One can only imagine the shock each attendee experienced as news of the Aggies' stunning victory was later learned.

And so I missed the most exciting ending of the most unforgettable Texas A&M victory in a lifetime—ever. But I wasn't the only one.

That gaggle of sportswriters up in the press box who had scampered into the elevators at the 4:15 mark emerged from the elevators to find Rice Stadium in a full roar. It was a wild, crazy celebration. Those Rice–A&M stories that had already been filed had to be rewritten. Much crow had to be hastily consumed. And Coach Bryant used that magnificent occasion to remind the squad that they should never, ever give up.

The victory was especially sweet for Coach Bryant and his fine coaching staff. Traditionally, opposing coaches meet at midfield for postgame pleasantries. I always had a hunch that the hand-shaking after that game was brief and not that cordial. Coach Neely did not like Coach Bryant, and the feeling was mutual.

Chapter 24

Dennis Goehring

Mr. Junction Boy

Coach Bryant, after he left Aggieland, heaped praise upon Dennis Goehring by calling him one of his favorite players who managed to survived Junction. He was described as one of the "biggest of the smallest" guards Coach Bryant had ever coached. In an interview with Gabe Bock on Texags.com, Goehring recalled meeting with Coach Bryant that first spring training session in 1954. The posted player roster showed him as a guard on the last-place team.

And Goehring was pretty hot about it. He met with Coach Bryant and demanded to know if he had a scholarship for the coming year or not.

Bryant's response was blunt. He told Goehring, "No, I don't want you on the team. You're not a football player."

That provoked Goehring, who confessed to having a hair-trigger anger, to jump out of his chair and lean menacingly over Coach Bryant's desk. Goehring pounded his fist on the desk and countered, "Okay, you SOB, you let me come back this fall, and if I make the team, you give me a scholarship. If I don't, you can kick me off the team."

Bryant said, "Okay. You've got a deal." Goehring later theorized he had managed to either catch Coach Bryant at a good time or he simply felt he could run Goehring off that fall anyway.

As Junction moved along, there came a time when Goehring was having his ankles taped before practice and, as an added element of protection, having his fists taped as well. At Junction, daily fights were inevitable. A guy would move up the chart if he won those battles.

Smokey Harper ambled over while the taping was underway and told Goehring that Coach Bryant felt it was time to give it up. It was time to quit because Coach Bryant wanted him to quit.

In John Underwood's well-written book *Bear,* Goehring is quoted as saying, "I'll be here when you and Bryant are both gone." I have it on good authority that Goehring's response was a little saltier than Underwood's recollection. Fact is, I know what Goehring actually said because he told me. Goehring also told me that one of the most difficult challenges he faced was the time he had to ask if Coach Bryant would consider offering his younger brother, Allen, a football scholarship.

Bryant asked for a rundown on the younger Goehring's assets. Size? Weight? Speed? Check, check, check. Finally, Coach Bryant asked, "Is he meaner than you?"

Goehring answered, "Definitely!"

Coach Bryant then said, "Great! I want him!"

Some years after Coach Bryant left, Goehring was seeking investors for the Bank of A&M, and he reached out to Coach Bryant to see if he would be interested in becoming an investor. Goehring was president of the new bank. He told Coach Bryant, "If you can buy 200 shares, I will be happy."

Coach Bryant paused—as Goehring theorized he should have only asked for 100 shares—and then Bryant said, "Give me 1,000 shares." That represented a $30,000 investment, and Goehring proudly points to the fact that when the bank was eventually sold to a new group a few years later, Coach Bryant's shares were valued at $70,000.

Goehring was a US Air Force guy, a pilot. He declined an offer from Coach Bryant to coach at Alabama and instead honored his contract with Uncle Sam and flew as a B-57 pilot in the Strategic Air Command. His younger brother, Allen, proved to be an outstanding player as he followed in the elder Goehring's footsteps. While flying his fighter jet in Japan, he experienced a flameout and, as opposed to exiting his aircraft over a populated area, flew it into the side of a mountain. It was a heroic move, to say the least.

Goehring was certainly on target with his prediction that he would be around College Station long after both Harper and Bryant were gone. Both Bear and Smokey are deceased, of course, but Goehring is both semiretired and still plugging along and functioning effectively on behalf of Bryan–College Station with the Bryan Business Council.

What I can best recall about both of the Goehrings was that they were “good guys”: rock-solid, caring, terrific teammates, and definitely guys you want to have on your side when a fight breaks out.

“When the going gets tough, the tough get going.” That would be the Goehring boys.

Chapter 25

The Aggies Are Back!

Gene Stallings joined Coach Paul Bryant at Alabama after graduating from Aggieland and served as an assistant coach for six seasons. He later was named head football coach at his alma mater, Texas A&M, when he was only twenty-nine.

Stallings was first known from his youthful days in Paris, Texas, as "Bebes." It was a family nickname that stuck, and his coaches and teammates also called him Bebes. He emerged from his year as one of the Junction Boys as a potential head coaching candidate by Coach Bryant.

In Stallings's seven seasons in Aggieland, he had but one winning season. This story is about that one special 1966 season at Texas A&M. Stallings had—finally!—recruited and assembled a talented squad of athletes who showed great promise. However, all roads to the Southwest Conference championships ultimately and typically ran through Austin.

That summer before the season began, Bebes and I had a couple of productive conversations about his coming season's weekly TV show. At that time, I was an account supervisor at McCann-Erickson in Houston. McCann-Erickson was the long-serving advertising agency for Humble Oil & Refining Company, the sole sponsor of the Southwest Conference football games on statewide radio networks. Humble aired every game in the Southwest Conference every season for more than thirty-five years, and the huge statewide audience knew the top game each week would be broadcast by the No. 1 announcing team of Kern Tips and Alec Chesser.

Tips was a vice president at McCann-Erickson, and even though he sought to remain impartial, he considered Texas A&M to be one of his personal favorites and recalled fondly the two occasions when he spent time interviewing Coach Bryant. He wrote a book called *Football, Texas Style* and referenced his admiration for Coach Bryant's considerable coaching skills.

My role each fall of each football season was to serve as producer at one of the Southwest Conference games. That all changed for the 1966 season. Stallings asked if I might be available that season to direct and produce the *Gene Stallings Show*. This idea was submitted and approved by both Tips and Humble. I was also logged in to supervise each A&M radio broadcast.

As best I can recall, there were about a dozen television stations around the state that welcomed Coach Stallings's program. Typically, local Texas Aggie–related sponsors would opt in as advertisers for the weekly programs. It is interesting to point out the fact that Humble considered radio broadcasting of the Southwest Conference as a gesture of statewide good will. Only one thirty-second spot ran during each half and was delivered by the on-air play-by-play announcer. The weekly message was simple: "Be sure to stop in at your neighborhood Humble station next week and thank them for sponsoring these broadcasts." Every year, Humble would produce Southwest Conference pocket schedules for the SWC and one year offered specially imprinted glasses.

Mickey Herskowitz was the beat reporter assigned to cover the Texas Aggies, and the *Houston Post* gave him permission to additionally serve as moderator of the *Gene Stallings Show*, along with Stallings. They proved to be an effective two-man team. They had good on-air chemistry together.

We jointly determined that it would be a good idea to come up with a theme—a rallying cry, if you will—for the weekly thirty-minute telecasts. In light of the success evidenced by the assembly of a very talented team, it was agreed the team's theme would be "The Aggies are back!"

Each game was filmed, of course, and immediately after the game the reels would be hustled back to a film processor in Houston on Buffalo Speedway. The heart of each telecast would be a twelve-minute edited segment that carried the highlights of the game. Back in the 1950s, live telecasts were few and far between.

Each Sunday morning at 5:00 a.m., the crew would assemble at Channel 39 (then), and every effort would be made to produce a thirty-minute program in order to stay on schedule to deliver tapes of each broadcast to the airport (or an automobile). We maintained a rigid schedule to assure delivery on the receiving end in time for the first scheduled telecast. Many of the major stations aired the program on Sunday evening.

The set comprised two Herman Miller Eames chairs with a suitable backdrop and a table positioned in front of the two chairs. Early on, we determined we would use a Spalding J5-V football as our prop, and we utilized the creative design services of McCann's Jesse Caesar to carefully hand-cut white plastic lettering that said "The Aggies Are Back!"

As the season began to move closer, we realized it might be a good idea to have a different message on the other side of the football. After all, what might happen if and when we lost? At the time, guys who earned T-Association letters received white sweaters with a maroon block *T*—nothing more. The same maroon block *T* was featured on white baseball caps.

Jesse Caesar should rightfully be credited with successfully adding an *A* and an *M* in close proximity to the *T*. This was a time when computers were not available to resize and manipulate type. Simply stated, the capital *A* and the capital *M* were not exactly equal in design or type font value: the *A* was not as wide as the *M*. Nonetheless, Caesar worked on it and creatively delivered a handsome prop football that had "The Aggies Are Back!" on one side and the *T* with an *A* and *M* positioned immediately below the serifs of the block *T*. This was, to the best of our knowledge, the very first time the *aTm* logo was used.

We were all set for the season to begin. The first game was against a talented Southern Methodist team on Kyle Field. It was a nationally televised contest and—miracle of miracles!—the Aggies scored late in the fourth quarter to take the lead. But then a superstar in the making named Jerry LeVias snagged a Mustang touchdown pass as time expired, and the Aggies were outscored by SMU, 20-17. LeVias was one of the first African Americans to play in the Southwest Conference. And he was a dandy!

That first Sunday taping session after that opening game was a sobering event. The Aggies were not back. The telecast opened with the football featuring the block *aTm*.

The buzz those days was that this was, finally, an Aggie team that was destined to make things happen. But the next games went like this:

Game 2: Purdue 24, Texas A&M 20
Game 3: LSU 17, Texas A&M 6
Game 4: Florida State 19, Texas A&M 18

Thus, through the first four games of the 1967 season, the Aggies stood at 0-4. And then the first miracle occurred. In a hard-fought contest on a Saturday night in Lubbock, the Texas Tech Red Raiders scored late in the fourth quarter to take the lead. But with the clock ticking down to zero, Edd Hargett, the Aggie quarterback, sought an open receiver from about the Tech 20-yard line and, when everyone was covered, zig-zagged his way into the Red Raiders' end zone. He actually crossed the goal line as the clock was counting down to 0:00. Finally, the Aggies won a game: Texas A&M 28, Texas Tech 24.

Still, the opening of the next show featured the block *aTm* football. Then in subsequent weeks the Aggies reeled off victories against TCU, Baylor, Arkansas, and Rice. Only the Texas Longhorns stood in their path on the way to the Southwest Conference football championship.

The game was held in Austin, and, in the end, the Aggies bested their No. 1 rival, 10-7. It was on the Sunday after that immense Saturday victory that the prop football was—finally!—turned around. "The Aggies Are Back!" Finally, it was a true statement.

One final, unanticipated episode telecast was subsequently staged in preparation for the Cotton Bowl game, which featured as the opponent—you guessed it—Coach Bryant's University of Alabama Crimson Tide.

It was like a dream come true for Stallings. And for Bryant! He was Stallings's former head coach at Texas A&M and his mentor when he coached at Alabama—his dear friend who first realized the fantastic future that was in store for Gene "Bebes" Stallings.

It was a helluva game, but the Aggies beat Alabama 20-16, and after the game a very proud Coach Bryant hoisted Stallings onto his shoulder at midfield. They both celebrated as they marched off the Cotton Bowl playing field together.

Coach Bryant was invited by Stallings into the Aggies' dressing room. Bryant told Stallings, "I don't want to talk to you. I want to talk to your players." And that he did. He knew every player's name without an introduction, and he personally congratulated each and every Aggie. What a special once-in-a-lifetime moment for Gene Stallings and Texas A&M.

There are a couple of postscripts that need to be mentioned. The Texas Aggies' football helmet carried a version of our prop football's *aTm*, but it was theorized that the helmet provider simply took note of the football prop and did their best to duplicate the "prop" design effort. That theory supports what happened next.

The following February, I received a letter from the general counsel at Texas A&M, asking if we could provide the football that was used in the television program. I had latched onto it myself as a keepsake but ultimately accepted the payment of $150 offered for the football and, by extension, the rights to the design of the *aTm* on that prop. I cashed the check and gave $75 to my dear friend, Jesse Caesar.

That logo is now valued in the tens of millions of dollars—and we sold it for $150! Maybe not my best-ever business decision. As for the prop football, who knows where it is today? It was once a featured item in the Texas A&M Football Museum, but that facility is long gone, and so is the ball, I suppose.

Truly, Gene Stallings made things happen while at Texas A&M. It was a grand and glorious time, and it traced its roots back to the hot, dusty practice fields at Junction, Texas, where Coach Paul Bryant realized that Bebes Stallings was just one of his winners on that famous squad of players.

Chapter 26

Charlie Caldwell from Krueger

Back in the mid-1950s, there really weren't that many press conferences on college campuses. "Pressers" is what they are called today. But not too many weeks after Coach Bryant arrived in College Station in the spring of 1954 to take over the reins of the Aggie football wagon, there was a called gathering of the usual media suspects, which included Mickey Herskowitz, Charlie Carder, and one or two of the local news guys, hosted, for want of a better word, by Jones Ramsey. From time to time, the *Fort Worth Star-Telegram* would send a writer down to the Brazos Valley, but that particular newspaper didn't hold Coach Bryant's Aggies in high regard.

The subject of this particular day was recruiting; there was no question about it. Coach Paul Bryant swooped into Texas and scooped up dozens of athletes eager to play for the man who left Kentucky to seek greener, more appreciative pastures. There was no limit to the number of recruits in those days.

Coach Bryant had committed most of the new recruits' names to memory, but he stumbled a bit when he wanted to introduce the guy who was probably the top lineman prospect in the state. Bryant proudly announced, "We've got a commitment from Charlie Caldwell from Krueger."

The locals looked at each other and laughed softly. And I think it was Jones Ramsey who whispered to Coach Bryant, "That's Charlie Krueger. He's from Caldwell."

Caldwell, of course, was very close to the Texas A&M campus, and Krueger was welcomed by all the new recruits because his reputation had preceded him. Any running back would be thrilled to run behind a guy like Charlie Krueger.

Without launching off into a totally different direction, this is an appropriate time to point out these were young high school athletes, and the weights of the players were substantially less than would be found in today's crop of top high school prospects. Krueger weighed in at between 215 and 220, and that happened to be pretty close to John David Crow's checking-in weight. Everyone knew Coach Bryant and the coaching staff paid close attention to the weekly weight list posting.

Crow once confessed he always checked Charlie Krueger's weight first and posted his weight afterward. If Crow weighed more than Krueger, Crow feared he might be shifted to the line, which was an absurd possibility, of course. But John David Crow was just as new as those other freshman players, and he felt uncomfortable taking a chance that he might outweigh Krueger.

What did Krueger accomplish during three seasons at Texas A&M? He was All-American twice and was eventually inducted into the College Football Hall of Fame in 1982.

Krueger was an affable fellow who was both well liked and respected by his teammates. He didn't scream and yell. He led by example and he was quiet about it. Coach Bryant preferred a more vocal leader, but that wasn't Krueger's style.

But there was one event that occurred and was shared with the Class of '58 at their fiftieth reunion in *Then and Now*, the yearbook commemorating that occasion. It went like this.

During the summer before the 1955 season, Jack Pardee, Gene Stallings, Don Watson, Jim Wright, Bobby Joe Conrad, and Stan Roper worked in the oil fields near Sinton. They worked every day from 7:00 a.m. to 4:00 p.m., and then they worked out later as a group for football. Some afternoons they would take notice of a car that was parked under a tree beside the football field, occupied by what appeared to be a couple of coaches.

One afternoon the car pulled up, and Coach Jim Owens and Coach Tom Tipps exited the vehicle and approached the group on the field. By the somber looks on their faces, the group sensed they were on a serious mission of some sort. They learned from the coaches that word had made it back to College Station that Charlie Krueger had left his job in Houston and was in Kingsville, where it was reported he planned to enter Texas A&I (now Texas A&M–Kingsville) in the fall. Owens coached the tackles, and he had been particularly tough on Charlie in the spring. Owens wanted some of the players to go to Kingsville, which wasn't that far from Sinton, to talk with Charlie and see if he couldn't be convinced to reconsider his decision to enroll at Texas A&I.

Five players volunteered to drive from Sinton to nearby Kingsville. As the chock-full car arrived at the athletic dorm, they were both surprised and elated to see Krueger exiting the dorm with a big smile on his face. Right alongside was Dennis Goehring, also sporting a huge grin. Charlie proudly announced, "I am coming back! Let's go get a beer!"

The coaches had reached out to Goehring, who lived near Krueger on C Ramp in Walton Hall. They had become close friends, and Goehring helped Krueger as he pondered the gravity of his situation.

Charlie was ultimately selected to most of the All-America teams and also was invited to play on both Hula Bowl and Senior Bowl teams. What is remarkable about many of those players is they often played the entire game without a substitute cycling in for relief. That "once you leave in a quarter, you cannot come back in" was a tough rule.

Charlie was a first-round selection in the 1958 draft and was the eighth player selected. He played defensive tackle for fifteen seasons with the San Francisco 49ers. He was a two-time Pro Bowl selection (1960, 1964) and was twice named Second-Team All-Pro (1960, 1965). The 49ers retired his No. 70 jersey.

At age fifty-one in 1988, Krueger was awarded more than $2.3 million in damages stemming from a lawsuit against the San Francisco 49ers. The judge on the case found that Krueger received repeated anesthetic injections during his NFL career so that he could continue to play in spite of significant knee injuries. The decision found that the 49ers were not truthful with Krueger regarding the seriousness of his injuries, which left him with severe chronic pain after his playing days.

Charlie Krueger—not Caldwell—now lives in retirement in northern California. He weighed 217 when he first signed the weight sheet at Texas A&M in the fall of 1954. He retired at a svelte 256. Charlie Krueger is fondly remembered by his teammates. He was, truly, one of the "good guys" you always hear about.

Chapter 27

John David and Bobby Joe

John David Crow, while later serving as athletic director at Texas A&M after a highly successful playing career—mostly with the Chicago Cardinals, the St. Louis Cardinals, and the San Francisco 49ers in the NFL—shared a recollection from that period when, for the spring training season of the University of Alabama football team, he functioned as an assistant coach at the invitation of Coach Bryant.

Coach Bryant, knowing full well the experience Crow brought to the occasion, simply suggested he spend his time watching and evaluating. If and when he saw something that needed correcting by a player, he was encouraged to be an active coach. The opening on the staff occurred because the fellow who traditionally coached the backfield—an Alabama assistant athletic director—coached the Bama track team in the spring.

Coach Bryant positioned the opportunity this way: "You'll find out if you want to coach. And I will find out if you can coach." In so many ways, this was a favor extended by Coach Bryant. Crow was a Heisman Trophy winner in 1957, and he was considering future options. Returning to the college-level practice field was certain to evoke many fond memories.

Near the end of practice, as Crow was watching the on-field action, he suddenly was aware that Coach Bryant was standing at his side. Coach Bryant had a way of draping a massive arm over your shoulders, a gesture that assured rapt attention. Bryant was a giant of a man—in so many ways—but even though Crow was also "super size," Bryant's size was impossible to ignore.

Bryant then said, "You know, John David, if only I had been smart enough to put Bobby Joe [Conrad] at quarterback and put Richard Gay at fullback, we would have won every game."

Crow said, before he could help himself, "Well, Coach. If you'd just let Bobby Joe kick field goals, we would have won all the games anyway." At that hold-your-breath moment frozen in time, Crow said he felt the weight of Coach Bryant's arm suddenly lift off his shoulders. And he wondered just how badly his comment might have been received.

With no further conversation on this topic indicated, Crow said he immediately set his sights on the door to the coach's dressing room and wondered if he could make it that far without breaking into a run. He knew he had touched a sensitive topic. Nonetheless, he briskly made his way to the locker room, where he showered and dressed and tried to convince himself that his commentary would not be harshly judged. After all, he needed Coach Bryant's support wherever he landed.

The way it turned out? Crow first accepted a slot as an assistant coach at Alabama and later served as an assistant coach with the Cleveland Browns and the San Diego Chargers. Prior to coming back to Texas A&M, he functioned as both head coach and athletic director at Northeast Louisiana University.

How did he land at Texas A&M? Jackie Sherrill, then athletic director and head coach at A&M, realized the potential value Crow represented for Texas A&M. So in 1983 he offered Crow a job as an associate athletic director at Texas A&M. Sherrill said, "I knew John David was a good fit for the job in College Station. He could help in a lot of ways that no one else could. And he did." When Sherrill departed in 1988, Crow succeeded him and held that position for more than four years. He served as director of athletic development until retiring in 2001.

But let's back up for a moment and introduce the relevance of Bobby Joe Conrad in this impromptu history lesson. Both Crow and Conrad ended up starting their professional careers with the Chicago Cardinals. Conrad had been initially drafted by the New York Giants but was subsequently traded to the Cardinals, where he functioned that first season as a defensive back. In 1959 both he and Crow played in the same backfield.

Of course, Crow and Conrad had frequently shared time in the Aggies' backfield as varsity teammates. Had you queried all of the Aggie players as to who was the most versatile athlete on the team, Conrad would probably have won hands down.

The records will show that Loyd Taylor was Texas A&M's go-to guy for extra points and field goals during his varsity years. Taylor was both reliable and consistent. Everyone knew Conrad had an even stronger leg, and there were so many who felt he could have won that final game against Rice because of his stronger leg. Unfortunately, Conrad had been on the field earlier in the fourth quarter, so he was ineligible to come back on the field for a shot that might have won the game.

But Bobby Joe Conrad never attempted a field goal while at Texas A&M.

And remember: Texas A&M lost three straight games at the end of the 1957 season against Rice, Texas, and Tennessee, and just one field goal per game would have done the trick.

Now that we have established Crow's connection with both Bryant and Conrad, here's another tidbit. John David Crow credited Coach Bryant with his always being called "John David." Without Bryant's assist, he would have been known as John or David or J. D. Funny how things work out.

Bobby Joe Conrad was another one of those two-name guys. He came to College Station from nearby Clifton and had the distinction of being named an All-State quarterback for a team that won their district championship two years in a row—in 1952 and 1953. As a senior, he scored an impressive 207 points. It is generally accepted that Bobby Joe Conrad was the most versatile athlete on the Texas A&M team. He was athletically gifted. He was a superb basketball player. He ran track. I don't know if he played golf, but if he did, I'd have wagered he would have considered shooting par as an easy goal. Add to the equation the fact that he was an excellent student and was very well liked by his teammates.

After graduation, both Crow and Conrad ended up as teammates for the Chicago Cardinals (later the St. Louis Cardinals). At the end of the 1957 football season at A&M, Conrad found himself tabbed as a member of the College All-Stars and participated in an exhibition game against the NFL champion, the Detroit Lions. All Conrad did in that game was kick four field goals and three extra points—and he intercepted a pass!—as the College All-Stars beat the Lions. It was an amazing performance. Conrad's NFL career was off to a flying start.

Conrad was selected in the fifth round of the NFL. He was the fifty-eighth player selected, and during his professional career that lasted eleven years, he was named to both the All-NFL team (1963) and the Pro Bowl (1964). After football, he returned to Clifton and was elected county judge, a position he held for many years. He now lives in retirement in Clifton. But if you stopped him on the street and asked him about that time Coach Bryant ended a difficult practice as the team was preparing to play Rice, I am sure he would recall that experience vividly.

It has already been established that Coach Bryant harbored a distaste for anything related to Rice. The Owls were always a tough opponent. On this occasion, it was probably a late Tuesday afternoon on Kyle Field. The team most frequently practiced behind Kyle Field. This time, they were on Kyle Field.

This late in the season, the turf was pretty badly chewed up. Practice did not go well. Busted plays. Dropped balls. And it was cold, wet, and dismal as the skies darkened. Finally, with disgust, Coach Bryant called a halt to the practice and sent the team to the warm, dry locker room. A difficult practice had mercifully ended.

As the team headed for the tunnel that connected Kyle Field to the locker room, Coach Bryant looked at me and said, "Not you." So there we both stood. The Kyle Field lights were on. The rain was making an effort to turn into sleet. The wind was whistling through, and Coach Bryant was smoking a cigarette.

After about ten minutes of silence between us, he told me to go to the locker room and tell the team to come back onto the field. Practice was about to restart.

As I entered the locker room, I saw most of the team had already shed their wet uniforms. They were not happy with the news I delivered from Coach Bryant. I had to relay the news to John David Crow, who was in the showers at the time. As you might expect, none of the guys were pleased with the order to get back on the field.

As practice resumed, the team shifted from "horizontal" to "vertical." In other words, the team practiced between the sidelines. Order was quickly restored and practice resumed.

But what hadn't changed was the weather, which was growing more dismal by the minute. Finally, a wide sweep play to the right was called, and I am pretty sure it was Loyd Taylor carrying the ball. As he sought to round the end, he had a ferocious collision with Carlos Esquivel. Brutal hit! So hard that both players threw off their helmets and squared off.

They circled. They clenched their fists. But neither threw a punch. It was just too damned cold to add to the problem by hitting a teammate. Someone laughed. Coach Bryant, realizing the message he sent had been well received, ended practice, and the team rushed back into the locker room.

In John Underwood's book, *Bear*, Crow confessed that this was a day when he came very close to quitting. Bryant was testing Crow with that ploy of ordering the team back onto the field. Bryant later said he asked Crow why he didn't quit that day. And Crow said, "Because I would have killed you before I'd let you make me quit."

On a closing note, it saddens me to realize Crow, Esquivel, Dudley, Marks, and Stanley, among others, are all gone. What a hoot it would be to ask for their recollections of that dismal day on Kyle Field when Coach Bryant decided to test John David Crow.

Chapter 28

Spur's Favorite Son

Bob Walker was a proud Spur Bulldog. He graduated from Spur High School in the spring of 1954 and immediately finalized arrangements to attend a six-week course schedule at Junction, which we all know was the site of the first training camp for Coach Paul Bryant's first Texas A&M varsity team.

A little background is both relevant and revealing. Spur, even then, was a tiny town out in Dickens County, just south of the Panhandle. It earned its name by virtue of the fact that a part of the fabled Spur Ranch was within the town's boundaries. Even today, the population hovers around 1,000, and the only other person from Spur who has achieved worldwide fame and recognition is Billy Joe "Red" McCombs, who amassed a huge fortune in any number of endeavors.

Young Walker knew he was potentially at a scholastic disadvantage, being unprepared for a rigorous classroom regimen. Spur had good schools and good teachers, but there were gaps that might ultimately come into play. Walker and his family felt it made sense to enroll at the Texas A&M Adjunct, a summer school in Junction where incoming freshmen could take basic first-year courses.

Walker made A's and B's in Spur, but he said a small-town school did not prepare him for what awaited him at A&M. He reports, "They said, 'You have to take a slide course.' I had never seen a slide rule. I had no idea what that was."

It was while Walker was at Junction that Aggie football came to town. History tells us the varsity squad arrived in three buses, and although there were only ten days of practices, the competition was so difficult and the competitive standards so high that only about one-third of the squad survived Junction and only one bus was needed to return the Texas A&M team back to College Station.

Even though practices were relatively closed, Walker did see the team practicing on the hot, dusty field that had far more sandburs than blades of grass. Walker had set his sights on becoming an electrical engineer and, like most young Aggies entering Texas A&M, he had to first know if he could achieve passing grades in that major. As things turned out, he and the EE Department agreed that electrical engineering would not be a good fit.

Walker next shifted to architecture—for any number of good reasons—but soon grew bored with the classroom routines. After struggling with a few courses in that curriculum, he realized he just might be better prepared to do something else and shifted his focus to marketing.

Walker was a superb sales person. He helped finance his college days by selling Bibles, cookbooks, and dictionaries door to door in West Virginia. As his selling skills improved, he shifted to selling insurance and began his career after graduation in 1958, raising funds for Pepperdine University in Los Angeles. He was a natural-born fundraiser.

Walker had met and subsequently married JoAnn Nolen in 1958 while at A&M. They married in the All Faiths Chapel on campus and were married fifty-two years before she passed away. Walker said this about JoAnn, "My sweet wife was the most understanding lady in the world. I give her all the credit for being able to take care of things at home. I had to travel." And travel he did. As a primary fundraiser for Pepperdine, he would typically travel nearly 100 days each year.

Flashing forward to 1966, Walker was elated to learn Coach Paul Bryant would be one of the featured speakers at Pepperdine's annual summer coaching clinic. That particular year the agenda featured three national champion coaches. The impressive roster included Rod Dedeaux, who won eleven national championships while coaching the University of Southern California baseball team. Then there was John Wooden, who coached the UCLA basketball teams that won ten national titles. At the top of the list, however, was Coach Paul Bryant, who won six national titles while at the University of Alabama. (And one Southwest Conference championship at Texas A&M in 1956!)

The Pepperdine athletic director knew Walker was a Texas Aggie and—on top of that—enjoyed a cordial relationship with Coach Bryant from their early days at Junction. Accordingly, he invited Walker to join him one morning for breakfast at the head table where the first featured speaker was to be Coach Bryant.

Walker recalled the event was staged in a banquet hall that would hold a crowd of 1,000 or more, and the speaker's elevated platform, where the guest speakers were seated, stood about three feet higher than the main floor and was carpeted.

Coach Bryant, wearing a lapel microphone and holding a wax pencil for his X's and O's, stood before an overhead projector. He began his talk with a funny story, which made everyone laugh, but—just then!—he put his hand on his forehead and said, "Is there a doctor in the house?" Bryant fell backward and lay sprawled out on the floor. Most immediately thought he must have suffered a heart attack.

Walker revealed he had interviewed Coach Bryant earlier that morning in order to provide the athletic director with appropriate details that he could use in his introduction of Coach Bryant. In retrospect, Walker shared his recollection that Coach Bryant had appeared as if he had been in a war of some kind! The truth, he later pieced together, was that Coach Bryant had been in Las Vegas, enjoying his free time gambling. For three days!

This was one of those "What happens in Vegas stays in Vegas" moments. Walker was seated in the front row next to the Pepperdine track coach, who immediately leapt to Coach Bryant's aid and said, "Call Dr. William Allen!" Dr. Allen was a dear friend of the Pepperdine athletic director. He was also the man who had delivered the Walker family's four children. They were close friends. They attended church together.

When Walker reached him on the phone, he said, "I have an ambulance that will be there in five minutes. I will meet you over at Morningside Hospital." John Underwood, a *Sports Illustrated* writer, was on assignment with Coach Bryant and rode alongside Walker in the ambulance on the way to the hospital.

A quick check of Coach Bryant revealed that he had not suffered a heart attack. He was, however, totally exhausted. Walker recalls Bryant telling him, "Bob, I am so sorry to let you down and also for passing out." Bob sought to assure Bryant their concern was for his health; not the coaching clinic.

Bryant was hospitalized at Morningside Hospital for four days. During that time Walker set up a press room down the hall and soon was fielding dozens of calls from friends and former players like Joe Namath, Coach Bebes Stallings, and John David Crow. Aggies and Crimson Tide players from all across the country—even Governor George Wallace!—were all voicing concern. Governor Wallace offered the immediate use of his private airplane if it was needed by Coach Bryant.

The next morning Coach Bryant's wife, Mary Harmon, arrived and would spend the remaining time with her husband. More tests were performed, and Coach Bryant's condition improved steadily. As Walker recalled on that first day at the hospital, Coach Bryant removed his watch and his championship ring from the 1965 season along with a sizable roll of $1,000 bills and his wallet from his pocket. By that time, an incredible number of floral displays were lining the hallways leading to Coach Bryant's room.

About the third day, Walker recalls, Coach Bryant said, "Bob, doesn't Dr. Allen attend your church?"

Walker said, "Yes, sir, he does."

Bryant then said, "Bob, I'd like for you to have all of these flowers delivered to your church in his honor. He has truly been a wonderful doctor for me."

It took several panel trucks making several trips to fulfill that request.

That last day, Dr. Allen walked in while Coach Bryant was dressing and said, "Coach, do you have any grandchildren?"

Bryant said, "Yes, I do."

"Would you like to see them grow up?"

Bryant replied, "Yes, sir, I would."

Dr. Allen then said, "Well, my advice would be to get rid of those Chesterfields and the alcohol. You need to take better care of yourself."

And Coach Bryant replied, "I plan to do that."

Coach Stallings subsequently recalled that Bryant did eliminate both activities for a few months or so, but then resumed his former practices. The doctors in Alabama strongly recommended he not schedule any speaking engagements for a year in order for his body to regain strength and stamina.

It was about six months later that Coach Bryant called the athletic director and asked if Pepperdine was once again going to conduct the annual coaching clinic. The answer was "Yes!"

Bryant then said, "Well, I am coming back out there, and I am bringing my offensive and defensive coordinators, and I am picking up the tab for the whole thing. I let you guys down last summer, and I want to make it up to you."

He came. They did a terrific job. And everyone was so pleased to have a happy, healthy Coach Bryant on stage with the key members of his coaching staff. These special moments were shared some time ago when so many interviews were being conducted for this book.

Dr. Bob Walker retired at the age of seventy-eight after nobly serving Texas A&M for forty-six years. His role as he departed was senior executive for development in the Office of the President of Texas A&M. While he was serving as a major fundraiser for Texas A&M, he generated hundreds of millions of dollars for his beloved school. He served under nine presidents at Texas A&M. Dr. Walker was honored as a Distinguished Alumnus in 2016.

His two rules that guided him—from the time he left Spur—were "Always tell the truth" and "Treat others the way you want to be treated."

Walker enjoys retired life in Bryan–College Station where he works in concert with his son Sid, Class of '82, in their rapidly growing fundraising consulting business. He has sufficient time, however, to enjoy Aggie sports and still manages to function effectively as class agent for the Class of '58. He makes sure to save some time for fishing. Dr. Bob Walker is truly one of the classiest members of a classy Class of '58.

Chapter 29

The Other Howard Payne

Texas A&M suffered the loss of a giant of a man on October 18, 2018. His name was Howard B. Payne, but everyone knew him as Buddy. He grew up in Houston and attended Austin High School. He was a member of the Class of '60 recruits who were drawn like a magnet to Texas A&M. Buddy was a good player for Coach Paul Bryant. Not great, but plenty good.

Like Jim Langston, he was not tall. But like Jim Langston, who was given the name "Round Man" by Coach Pat James, Buddy loved playing football for Texas A&M. He was smart. He was quick. And he loved striking a blow on the guy on the other side of the line of scrimmage. That was a quality that endeared him to Coach Bryant. Early on, he developed rock-solid friendships with a number of players on the team and with Joe Schmid, the '60 student manager.

The departure of Coach Bryant in late 1957 led to the naming of a new head football coach, Jim Myers, who came to Aggieland after a successful tour of duty at Iowa State University. Coach Myers's offense was the single wing, and that meant Buddy and his classmates were required to learn a totally different style of playing football. It was not a particularly fun time his final two years on campus.

But when it came to his studies, he was solid. Great grades and a congenial, positive, can-do attitude. He was also a leader and in his senior year was named commanding officer of B Athletics.

After his discharge from the US Army in 1962, Buddy joined Lynn Elliott Company, a sales and engineering company in Houston. He later acquired ownership of that company and expanded his business interests as he acquired several companies in the oil and gas industry. To say he succeeded would be a great understatement.

Buddy knew how to both acquire and manage new business, and he was a generous man. His love for Texas A&M spurred him to become actively involved in both the 12th Man Foundation and the Lettermen's Association. He served as president of both organizations and was inducted into the Texas A&M Lettermen's Hall of Honor in 2000. Back home, he served as president of the Houston Touchdown Club.

But there were other aspects of his life that are worth mentioning. His friendship and the mutually beneficial business opportunities that extended back to his playing days served to energize his entire life and business. He worked in concert with Charlie Milstead, Joe Schmid, Gail Oliver, and Joe Munson as they exchanged ideas and contacts to the benefit of all concerned. It was truly energizing to see the descendants of the Milstead and Payne clans involved in their respective family businesses as the years passed. The Milstead family called him "Uncle Buddy."

Buddy was quite active at Memorial Drive United Methodist Church, where he served in a variety of leadership roles for fifty-four years. His memorial service packed the chapel. More than two dozen Aggie teammates were present as they celebrated the life of a truly special person. They don't make many people like Buddy Payne. But the world sure could use a bunch of them!

Chapter 30

Jimmy Wright

Villanova and Such

When Coach Paul Bryant began recruiting talent for his first team at Texas A&M, Edinburg High School was one of the first schools he targeted. Edinburg had not one but two gifted athletes who had caught Bryant's eye.

The first was Jimmy Wright, a quarterback with a quick release and an accurate arm. The second was Carlos Esquivel, a shifty, fast halfback. Those two fine prospects had led their Edinburg Bobcats to the state semifinals. Why shoot for one when you can nab two?

The problem was, both were well targeted by most of the major colleges in the Southwest. Among the most ardent coaches pursuing Wright was Ed Price at the University of Texas. Price dreamed of having Wright in the UT backfield. If memory serves me correctly, the University of California had also extended offers to Wright.

Coach Bryant soon entered the competition for Wright—and Esquivel—and went so far as to share Babe Parilli's playbook with Wright. Parilli was the All-American quarterback for Coach Bryant when the Kentucky Wildcats won the unofficial national championship.

The competition was both fierce and constant. But in the end both Jimmy Wright and Carlos Esquivel cast their lot with the Texas Aggies and looked forward to hooking up with a very talented squad of teammates in Aggieland.

Wright was a Hollywood-handsome, blonde fellow with a big smile and a quick wit. It seemed like he was always tanned. Coach Bryant probably liked him because he had an outgoing personality. However, Bryant learned to love Wright most of all because he was not a quitter. And he was smart.

Wright found out he had to compete with some other very talented quarterbacks, including Bobby Joe Conrad, Roddy Osborne, and Donny Grant. In early practices the competition was both fast and furious—at the same time. Wright became aware that he had to become a productive player on both sides of the line of scrimmage.

Smokey Harper was hard of hearing, and Wright took great delight in bouncing into the training room before practice and, while having his ankles taped, talking in a very loud tone of voice. When that happened, Smokey would discreetly reduce the volume on his hearing aid, which he wore on a cord around his neck. As soon as Wright saw Smokey fiddling with his hearing aid, he would dial the volume back to slightly more than a whisper, and Smokey would have to make another adjustment. Fortunately, Smokey had a great sense of humor, and he certainly knew what Wright was doing. Smokey would also frequently squelch the volume if and when Coach Bryant walked in for a look-see.

It was Coach Bryant's belief that the quarterback had to be prepared to be the coach on the field. He mandated the quarterbacks' schedule—no classes after 2:00 p.m.—because he wanted to schedule regular meetings with the quarterbacks that began promptly at 2:15. Practice began each day at 3:00 p.m., but here's what Wright had to say one day on Texags.com:

> Every day for four years we met to go over the day's practice schedule. We had to know what our goals were for that day as a quarterback, the plays we were going to practice, the formations, the secondary, the coverages, the linebackers, blitzes, and end blitzes.
>
> Coach Bryant wanted us to be prepared. During the season, we would meet at his home and he would drill us over a pool table with a football field top on it. He would mark a spot on the field and give us down and distance and we would run through plays for that situation.

The first Kyle Field game in 1956 is worth mentioning. The opponent was Villanova, a pretty decent opponent from the East Coast. Wright was the designated starting quarterback in that game, which was played in front of a substantial Kyle Field audience.

Wright was playing well. Late in the first period, he targeted Loyd Taylor with a 30-yard pass that the fleet-footed Taylor ran into the end zone. Momentum immediately swung to the Aggies. As the game progressed,

Wright successfully connected a second time for another touchdown. At that point he was feeling pretty good about himself.

The Aggies were facing a fourth down with less than a foot to be gained for a first down at the Villanova 30-yard line. Wright *knew* the only play to call was a punt. But he quickly told the team in the huddle something along the lines of "To hell with that. We're going for it!"

And they didn't make it.

When Wright finished the long, long walk to the sideline after that play, a livid Coach Bryant told him he had played his last down for him and assured him he would never play quarterback again. He was banished to the bench for the rest of the game.

On Monday Wright mustered up the courage to go face to face with Coach Bryant and to declare there was "no way in hell" he was going to let Coach Bryant run him off the team. Wright stayed, of course. He spent some time gathering splinters on the bench, but he did play later on and he played well.

When an interviewer asked about this on TexAgs.com, he had this to say: "When Coach Bryant benched me, people didn't understand. I didn't become second team and quit, transfer, or leave. I wanted to help the team. You first want to help the team."

"Forgive and forget" is the phrase that leaps to mind.

One other Wright misadventure is worth revealing. Against Rice, Wright was again quarterback—and the designated punter—and there was a bright sun immediately overhead. The ball was near midfield.

Coach Bryant reminded Wright to kick the ball high to make the receiver field the punt while shading his eyes. Wright did kick it high, but it only carried about five yards past the line of scrimmage. Bryant yelled at him after the play, and Wright yelled back, "Yeah, you said to kick it high, but you didn't say how far."

Two quotes attributed to Coach Bryant seem worth mentioning insofar as his treatment of Wright was concerned. First, "I never give up on a player, regardless of his ability, as long as he never gives up on himself. In time, he will develop." And "When you make a mistake, there are only three things you should ever do about it: admit it; learn from it; and don't repeat it." Jimmy Wright was a talented, tough, smart quarterback with an upbeat attitude and a ton of football smarts.

Wright is retired and is a regular contributor to TexAgs.com. He lives in Bryan–College Station and continues to follow the Texas Aggies team closely. He is welcomed at all practices because he is, after all, Jimmy Wright.

Chapter 31

Odds and Ends

As we were searching and researching the various topics that might evolve into a full story, there were little snippets that came along that evoked a memory and a laugh. These are things guys remember that, like gnats in a deer blind, just won't go away.

One of those instances was reborn and chronicled in *Then and Now*, the fiftieth reunion yearbook of the Class of '58. It went like this.

The Aggies were playing the Arkansas Razorbacks at their home stadium in Fayetteville and had played poorly in the first half. The mood in the dressing room was somber, to say the least. Coach Bryant ordered everyone to leave the room. As everyone stood up to depart, Bryant corrected that misunderstanding by saying, "I mean everybody but me and the players."

I stayed. As everyone else filed out, Coach Bryant picked up a chalkboard and looked for a place to put it. The only place available was a small table that contained some training supplies and a stylish new Stetson hat that Coach Jim Owens, our head assistant coach, had just purchased. Coach Bryant took his giant hand and, with one swipe, cleared the table. The last thing Coach Owens saw as he exited the room was his beautiful Stetson hat floating on the filthy water of the dressing room floor. He did not dare go back to retrieve it.

After giving the team the plan for the second half, Coach Bryant stormed around the room, glaring at various players. When he came to Henry Clark, a senior guard, he grabbed Henry by the jersey, jerked him up out of his chair, butted him in the head, and said, "Henry, when are you going to hit someone?"

Fortunately, Henry was wearing his helmet. Unfortunately, Coach Bryant only wore his brown felt hat. The houndstooth fedora Bryant made famous had yet to come along. As blood trickled down Coach Bryant's nose, Henry exhibited a puzzled look and said, "Coach, I haven't been in the game."

That game ended in a 7-7 tie. Coach Bryant described the event as "like having to kiss your sister." He felt he had failed by not having the team ready to play well enough to win. He always took the blame for a loss. He always felt we could win any game because we had better mamas and papas. How could anyone argue with that premise?

The final vignette, if you don't mind my using a word that most Aggies don't understand, concerns Jim Stanley, a tough, strong guy who called the coal mines of Kentucky his home. The gang got together after attending the All-College Rodeo and decided to drop by Shiloh Hall for a cold beer—or two. In the house that evening there was a sizable contingency of frisky local farm boys, along with a few Bryan hoods, along with their cute little girlfriends. What better way to impress a gal than to pick a fight with an Aggie football player?

The fight, which was destined to happen in the first place, began after first locking the doors. The owner called the cops. Right about then, someone looked outside and saw our Jim Stanley inside a large circle of observers doing battle with one of the local farm boys. John Tracey, who hailed from Pennsylvania and was tougher than a boot himself, was standing at the edge of the circle with a farmer under each arm. As Jim would polish one off, John would push another in Stanley's direction.

The melee ended when someone came to their senses and strongly urged us to get back to campus. Stanley rode the entire trip back to Walton Hall hanging onto the driver's side door. As the cops pursued, the car full of footballers turned one final corner and Stanley dove through a hedge to escape the long arm of the law. He might have gotten away with it, but Stanley's shirt was left behind at Shiloh Hall, and that shirt landed on Coach Bryant's desk the following morning. The next day marked the beginning of Stanley's Day One in the Corps of Cadets.

So many stories left to share, so little time. Wonder what ever happened to the clay pits? Probably a Walmart parking lot by now.

Chapter 32

Rings around the Brazos

Some friendships are easier to grow than others. One great personal example of that premise is Willie Zapalac. I first met Coach Zapalac when I was a fish student manager. Coach Willie was an Aggie, and that set him apart from the other assistant coaches that Coach Bryant had recruited for his staff.

He was one of the easiest coaches to approach while at Texas A&M, and once he left College Station, he settled in with the Texas Longhorns and did an absolutely superb job. He was in Austin twelve years and the Longhorns went to eleven bowls in that period.

Our friendship continued to grow as both our jobs and lives changed. I was corporate communications manager for Dr Pepper/Seven-Up in 1955 and, through a friendship with Steve Hatchell, was able to secure lead sponsorship status for Dr Pepper as the new Big 12 Conference was formed. The American Football Coaches Association was headquartered in Waco, and there were periodic opportunities to both sponsor and participate in golf outings. Most of the coaches enjoyed playing golf. Some are really good, and the wild-and-crazy betting between well-heeled coaches can boggle the mind.

One beautiful spring afternoon at a fancy golf course outside of San Antonio, I found myself sharing a golf cart with Willie Zapalac. The other pair in our foursome included Spike Dykes, now long gone but then closely tied to Texas Tech. Spike was an absolutely hilarious guy. He had the worst swing you could ever begin to imagine, but the ball always seemed to go right down the middle of the fairway.

We had a lot of fun talking about the good old days, and Willie filled in many of the blanks that I had never known about his time at Texas A&M. As we were waiting for the guys ahead to tee off, Willie asked me if I knew about the rings. I pled ignorance, which is pretty easy for me to do.

Willie recalled there was a time right after the Texas Aggies won the Southwest Conference football championship in 1956 when the Board of Regents authorized the design and purchase of a SWC championship ring for each letterman. The team was on probation, and the ring would serve to ease the pain of being denied an invitation to the Cotton Bowl. Coach Bryant balked at the idea. It had taken him some time to understand and appreciate some of the traditions at Texas A&M.

These days Ring Day is a huge deal on campus. Back in the 1950s, there was no ceremony, but the Aggie ring is the one and only ring that is universally worn and treasured by Texas Aggies. So Coach Bryant's decision made sense. He didn't want the players to feel obligated to wear two rings, and he didn't want the championship ring to overshadow the Aggie ring. Case closed.

At this time, troubling signs were beginning to emerge with Coach Bryant and certain members of the Board of Regents. The way Willie told it, Bryant had been promised a paid-up annuity that had never materialized. And he didn't like that one bit.

The football coaches would typically gather at the Bryant household on Monday nights during the off-season to discuss coaching business, recruiting, and football. On this night, which was about two weeks away from the Texas A&M football banquet, Jack Daniels was the beverage and the spirits were spirited. At some point, Willie related, he asked Coach Bryant about the championship rings. They all knew he had nixed the idea with the regents, but nothing more was ever said about those rings.

Coach Bryant asked, "Would you like to see them?" He then retreated to his private office and returned with a tray of Texas A&M championship rings. They were beautiful, as you might imagine.

Willie then asked if they were going to be presented at the banquet, and Coach Bryant said, "Not on your life. I personally bought Southwest Conference championship watches, and those personalized watches are what we will be presenting to the Texas A&M team that night."

Here's where it gets interesting. Coach Bryant had a new Cadillac supplied each year, and he said, "Whoever wants to tag along, we're going to take a short trip!" As Willie reported it, they loaded up the Caddy and a couple of other cars and drove straight out to what all of us Aggies knew as "Whiskey Bridge" on the Brazos River. They took the bottle of Jack Daniels along for the ride and toasted winning that SWC title, and then Coach Bryant tossed the tray of rings into the Brazos River.

It was agreed that nobody would ever, ever mention that deed. This was to be the coaching staff's best-kept secret. The night of the Texas A&M banquet, when the time came to have each player step forward, each fellow received a personalized Southwest Conference championship watch. All were excited!

Those regents in attendance undoubtedly looked at each other in puzzlement. Either they failed to ask Coach Bryant about the rings or they simply did not want to ask that question. As far as I knew, nobody knew.

But there came a time when the Junction Boys decided to honor Coach Bryant, so they all chipped in and bought him a Texas A&M championship ring and presented it, as I can best recall, at an event in New York City.

Fast-forward a few years. When the 1956 team assembled to be a part of the celebration surrounding Coach R. C. Slocum's Texas A&M team in 1993, a separate dinner was arranged and hosted by Coach Bryant's son, Paul Jr. On a personal note, Coach Bryant had charged me, as a student manager, to make damned sure nobody watched our practices. That included eight-year-old Paul, who would come by after school. I would, as gently as I could, run him off. Coach Bryant assured me I was doing the right thing. Later in life, I apologized to Paul Jr., who laughed and said he knew I was only following orders.

After socializing with the Slocum team in the larger dining room of the Hilton, the 1956 team returned to a more relaxed setting to enjoy the remainder of the evening. Paul Jr. asked someone to close the doors to assure our privacy, and then he said he would like each and every person in the room to tell one story about their relationship with or some special memory of Coach Bryant, whom he called "Papa." It was an amazing, memorable event, with many laughs and many tears. How I wish there was a recording of that special evening!

As soon as all of the guests had spoken, Paul Jr. returned to the podium and told the group, "Papa had a very special place in his heart for all of you guys. He and Mama had a special room adjacent to their bedroom that was his 'Aggie Room,' and the walls were adorned with team pictures and all sorts of memorabilia from that four-year pilgrimage in College Station."

He acknowledged his father's treasuring of the Texas A&M championship ring that was given to him by the Junction Boys. It was his wish that he be buried wearing that ring.

He then paused. And paused.

And then he said, as he raised his hand to show the crowd, "But, you know, Papa didn't raise no fool. Here's that ring!"

The applause was thunderous.

The memory of that evening is indelibly etched in all of our treasured memories about a very special time we now recognize as the Bryant era.

That annuity thing? Here's what I understand happened. Apparently, after Coach Bryant left Texas A&M, he sought to recover that paid-up annuity that was never delivered. Certain members of the Board of Regents resisted, and an impasse seemed likely to be the end result of the wrangling. Coach Bryant did consent to having those funds used, instead, to provide scholarships for the descendants of the men on the three teams he coached while at Texas A&M. If a son or grandson or even a daughter or granddaughter enrolled, scholarship money would be available. If the lad played football, he would receive a full scholarship. If the kid was simply a student, he or she would each receive an equal share of the year's funding that was available. To the best of my knowledge, that scholarship provision is still intact.

If any of you ever have an opportunity to visit the University of Alabama's Paul W. Bryant Museum, be sure to stop by the Texas A&M Room. It will make your heart burst with pride.

Gig 'em!

Chapter 33

Goodbye, College Station!

It was a pleasant early Sunday evening on campus. To be precise, it was November 10, the day following a victory over SMU on Kyle Field. I was sports editor for *The Battalion* and had already knocked out the story that would be carried in Monday's edition. What a fabulously exciting time. The Texas Aggies were No. 1 in the nation and had but two games remaining on the regular season schedule. Life was good.

And then one of the fish cadets from the guard station on the ground floor tapped on my door on the fourth stoop and told me Coach Bryant had called and wanted to see me at Kyle Field—right now.

I guess it must be my nature to fear the worst while hoping for the best. Nonetheless, I hotfooted it over to Kyle Field and went straight to Coach Bryant's office. His light was on and the door was open. I had replayed the entire week in my head and tried to remember if there was anything I had written that might have caused Coach Bryant to call me in the early evening.

I was surprised when Coach Bryant smiled at me and waved me in. He asked me to close the door. I swallowed hard.

There had been times in the past year when I spent no more than a few minutes with Coach Bryant after picking up practice films in Houston. This was not one of those times.

Then I noticed there was a bottle of whiskey—Jack Daniels?—on his desk. He poured a drink and offered me the same. I accepted nervously.

After a short pause, he delivered his message, and here's the gist. He told me he had made a decision to return to the University of Alabama as head football coach. His alma mater—his "Mama"—had called him home, and he couldn't turn the school down.

What did this have to do with me?

He said he wanted to tell me "his side" of the story and asked me to write up that story and bring it back to his office the next morning. I was told I should simply slip a sealed envelope under his door.

I asked, "Why me and not Jones Ramsey, our publicity director?" Coach Bryant's answer was that he feared someone at Alabama would blurt out the news and it would absolutely devastate the team. We were scheduled to play the Rice Owls the following Saturday and, four days later, face off against the University of Texas.

He also said he couldn't share the news with his coaches, either, out of fear they would suddenly become more focused on their future employment plans than on preparing the team for the game against the Owls.

We chatted as he replayed the sequence of events and said he wanted to have his side of the story ready if and when Alabama breached the silence agreement. He thanked me for doing a good job reporting on the team's success, and we joked about his game tickets. We had shared the proceeds of those tickets for three seasons.

I stumbled back to my hole with the weight of the world on my shoulders. I typed and retyped for a couple of hours and, finally, completed the story he asked me to compose. As I recall, since I couldn't sleep, I went back to Kyle Field that night and slipped it under his door.

Monday came and went. I visited the team practice Monday afternoon, and Coach Bryant simply said, "Thanks." And that was it.

I'm pretty sure it was Tuesday evening when the news broke that caused the sports world to implode on Wednesday morning. As opposed to holding what is now called a presser, Coach Bryant gave his written response, and Jones gave it to Frank Manitzas, the Associated Press contact up in Dallas. The story ran pretty close to what I had written. I later received a letter from Manitzas, thanking us for cooperating with them.

All of the air went out of the team. Practices were not at all focused. Everyone was whispering as they all wondered, "What next?" The rumor mill was running full tilt.

That Saturday, Rice outscored A&M, 7-6. Four days later, the Texas Longhorns outscored A&M, 9-7. The team slipped to No. 4 in the nation. The reward for the team was a trip to the Gator Bowl, to play—wait for it!—Tennessee, which beat A&M, 3-0. The Texas Aggies finished the season ranked No. 8.

What a bummer! Three games, six points, and the beginning of the end for the Bryant era. But it was one fantastic ride while it lasted!

Chapter 34

Skipping Finals

Monday, January 13, 1958, was the beginning of what was then known as "Dead Week": the last week to cram before finals. That was the way it was then. Not at all sure how it is now.

Virtually all of my Texas Aggie cadet pals were cramming and sweating as they prepared for their finals. From my point of view, however, there were more important issues to consider than studies. Mainly, with Coach Paul Bryant's departure at the end of the 1957 season, Texas A&M was without a head football coach, and every single Aggie had this intriguing subject foremost in his mind.

I was laboring along as sports editor of *The Battalion*, a position that probably came my way because I had served as football manager for the previous three football seasons. I took a particular liking to serving as the point man in covering the frenzy that accompanied the hiring of a new football coach to succeed a man on the way to becoming a legend in his own time, Coach Paul "Bear" Bryant.

As finals were approaching, Coach Bryant was already busy recruiting his first batch of recruits for the University of Alabama. *The Battalion* was, at the time, reputed to be the last uncensored college publication in the land. That previous week, I had editorially nailed the Board of Regents with a rather nasty write-up for failing to follow their own rules in targeting prospects for consideration. A Faculty Athletic Selection Committee was supposed to consider, assess, and sift through all candidates and finally nominate its hand-picked choice to be Coach Bryant's successor. At the time I wrote that editorial, it occurred to me that I might have taken things a bit too far. Later in life, this was called pushing the envelope, right?

I could almost hear the sounds of knives being sharpened as the issue was going to press. The implications were huge! Don Burchard, who was then the head of the Journalism Department, told me he didn't know whether to congratulate me for my bravery or wish me good luck as I moved down Highway 6 and returned to Houston.

At this same time, the Board of Regents were all engaged, shall we say, in the search process. Almost to a man, each regent had a favorite candidate he wanted to personally advance. And we're talking about some of the heavyweight football coaching studs at that time. Navy's Eddie Erdelatz, UCLA's Red Sanders, Notre Dame's Frank Leahy, Michigan State's Hugh "Duffy" Daugherty, and Iowa's Forrest Evashevski. All five of these guys were on the regents' short list.

However, while our regents were scurrying around and making front-page headlines all over the place, the search dragged on into the seventh week and the Faculty Athletic Selection Committee's efforts had all but been ignored. Its search process had zeroed in on one young, highly regarded head coach prospect who seemed genuinely interested in the promising position in College Station that was up for grabs. His name was Jim Myers. He was thirty-six years old. And he had coached the Iowa State Cyclones to an outstanding season the previous fall. If there was ever such a thing as an up-and-comer, Coach Jim Myers fit that description.

Iowa State was then the traditional doormat of the Big 8 Conference, as it was then called, but Coach Myers's hard-nosed squad of overachievers finished 4-5-1 in the Big Eight, and that progress earned him Coach of the Year honors in the conference.

What an incredible dilemma! When Iowa State administrators sensed Texas A&M was sniffing around their guy, they promptly gave him a substantial boost in salary and a new contract. I also recalled they scrounged up a ball and chain, and everyone got a big kick out of seeing Coach Myers togged out in that piece of medieval hardware.

I recall it must have been sometime Wednesday when, feeling frustrated and not wanting to even begin to think about the upcoming week of finals, I thought it would be a good idea to let Coach Jim Myers know he was the kind of a guy the Corps of Cadets would love to have as the Texas Aggies' head football coach.

Coach Myers had inherited an Iowa State squad that finished a dismal 2-8 season when he first arrived in Ames to take charge. It was intriguing to note that Coach Myers had taken a squad of 110 to the first spring practice and trimmed it down to 38 by the time drills had ended. His offense was single wing, and that attack required faster, quicker, and more athletic players than were typical at the time. A change of pace hampered opponents as they pondered the best way to stop the single wing.

The split T was then in vogue, but it was UCLA's single wing that had earned the Bruins a national championship in 1954. And Coach Myers was a member of the UCLA staff at that time. Add to the equation a need for each player to go both ways. This was no easy task, that's for sure.

The training was difficult and physically demanding, but when the following season began, those hapless Iowa State Cyclones were chiseled and sleek and averaged fifteen pounds less, per man, than in the previous year. This brought to mind those memorable days in Junction and suggested an approach to which the current roster of Aggies could immediately relate.

But, alas, there was an atmosphere of doom and gloom on the campus, and it had nothing to do with the upcoming week of tests. As I can best recall through the mists of sixty-six years gone by so damned rapidly, I decided it might be a good idea to send Coach Myers a telegram, telling him that in spite of the stumbling and bumbling by our cadre of higher-ups, he truly was our kind of guy.

And so I banged out a telegram that said just that and then hustled on over to Duncan Hall for chow that evening. I was so very proud to put my name first on the telegram, and Jon Hagler, my dear friend and cadet colonel of the Corps, put his name right below mine, and a long line of cadets each plunked down a quarter for the privilege of signing that Western Union telegram.

In all, 2,229 Aggies signed the wire, and it measured eighty feet in length. It took a long, long time to both send and receive. I suspect that it might still be a record, but Western Union telegrams are long gone now, so we will never know. When you stop to realize the total enrollment was just a platoon or two over 6,000, that's a pretty impressive number for such a short period of participatory enrollment.

The telegram was delivered to Ames with considerable impact, and Coach Myers hurriedly explained to an anxious press (and to Iowa State) that he had no plans to leave to come to Texas A&M. I think it was about that time that both *Sports Illustrated* and *Life* magazines called to see what we were planning to do next.

The "school solution," a term I learned later in life when I was at the US Army School of Armor in Fort Knox, Kentucky, was to say we had finals on the near horizon and we simply wanted to make a point.

I had the right to remain silent, but I didn't have the ability. And so I blurted out, "We have other plans," and left everyone hanging.

As Hagler and I strolled back to the solitude of Dorm 2, we conspired and jointly hatched a preliminary plan to go for broke, so to speak. That plan included a plot to purchase two airplane tickets to Ames. We felt it was important to travel to Ames over the weekend to personally introduce ourselves to Coach Myers and underscore our support for his candidacy. Those who have come to know me over the years are not that surprised that I would do such an off-the-wall deed, but Brother Hagler is a brilliant trooper of another stripe altogether, and he's never been one who would dare to leap out of an airplane without first asking if we shouldn't be wearing a parachute. I was fully prepared to save Jon's career if and when it came to that decisive point.

These were the days when credit cards were nonexistent, if you can get your mind around that fact. So I wrote what would later become known as a hot check, and we finalized our plans to fly out of Houston on Saturday. With a stop or two along the way, we targeted our arrival for late Sunday afternoon. We stopped and overnighted in Kansas City at my grandparents' home and found them less than fully convinced that our risk-vs.-reward expectations outweighed the wisdom of taking our final exams as scheduled.

Sunday was an all-day travel day, and we were two pooped Aggies when we finally strolled into the Student Union building on the Iowa State campus to register for our room. On Saturday, as I can best recall, I had made contact with Dr. Chris Groneman, who headed up the faculty search committee, and told him we were en route to Iowa to personally meet with Coach Myers—that is, if he would agree to see us.

Dr. Groneman, who knew I had strongly and editorially supported the his committee, seemed to be somewhere between surprised and totally flabbergasted at our act that bordered on outrageous. I recall asking him if, by any chance, the committee would nominate Coach Myers for the vacant position if Myers ultimately agreed to accept the nomination. I truly had no idea whatsoever that it might actually happen. But that's why people gamble and hope/pray they roll a seven, right?

When we were signing in at the Student Union, the desk clerk inquired as to the nature of our business on campus. And although we were dressed in civvies garb, the white sidewall haircuts should have been a dead giveaway. We simply said we were there to see Coach Myers and left it at that. That reinforced an observation on the part of the desk clerk that we were prospective jocks, and when the time came to check out, we were told the charges had been paid by the Iowa State Athletic Department.

When we strolled into Coach Myers's office, it didn't take but a nanosecond for Coach Myers to connect the dots and realize we were the guys who sent that eighty-foot telegram on his desktop. We both made note of the ball-and-chain beside his desk.

He immediately canceled all of his calls and meetings and told his secretary he would be at his home. This was Monday, day one of finals. He hustled us out of his office in less than five minutes. When we arrived at his home, after first meeting his charming wife and accepting her generous offer of food and drink, we settled in and enjoyed becoming better acquainted.

Coach Myers was truly stunned that we had done what we had done. But he seemed to label our effort as brave and not necessarily stupid. Hagler's parents and my parents might not have agreed with him on that premise.

We had dragged along a current edition of *The Aggieland* and some issues of *The Battalion*, but he really wanted to know more about the roster of players Coach Bryant had left behind for his successor.

We had a stellar squad. These were talented, highly recruited guys I had known since I first walked onto the campus and became a student manager. So he felt comfortable with my player-by-player assessment and the prospects for an even brighter future with those guys. If there was ever to be such a designation as a blue chipper, we had a bunch of them.

Ever so slightly, I sensed his decision to remain at Iowa State just might not be that firm or final. Both Hagler and I had been pushing hard—very hard—for Coach Myers to buy into the idea of becoming Texas A&M's next head football coach. Finally, Coach Myers leaned forward and confessed, "You know, I really wanted that job. God, it would have been great!" His wife was there when he said it, and she nodded her head in concurrence.

Later in life we would realize this was a Kodak moment. And so I lobbed the next pitch right down the middle of the plate and said, "Well, if the Faculty Selection Committee offers to nominate you, will you allow it? All things considered?" I was aware that the salary and contract terms had already been generally agreed upon a few days before when the committee had been in contact with Coach Myers.

To my utter astonishment, he said, "Yes. But I will have to deny you two guys were ever here." Gulp.

Midway through that chilly, gray winter afternoon in a suburb of Ames, Hagler and I both shook hands with Coach Myers, and we both made the "lips zipped" gesture. When we arrived back at the Student Union, I called Dr. Groneman. He informed us that the news of our surreptitious visit to Ames was plastered across the front pages of both the *Houston Post* and the *Houston Chronicle*. Our secret, it turned out, was anything but a secret.

Checking out was a breeze.

Over the weekend we had succeeded in our efforts to reach others who truly cared about Texas A&M football and those who knew the Board of Regents better than we did. And when I hit Dr. Groneman with the $64,000 question—"Will you nominate Coach Jim Myers if he agrees he will accept the job?"—his answer was "Yes, we will. But I would strongly urge you and Hagler to get back to the campus as soon as possible. And do not—under any circumstances—talk to anyone about your trip."

Tuesday was not only day two of finals but a travel day as well. Our departure from Ames was complicated by the arrival of a huge snowstorm that grounded many flights across the middle of the country. But when night fell, Hagler and I each collapsed in our respective bunks at A&M. We did not sleep that well.

Each of us was greeted back at our holes with a small note inside a small envelope from Dr. M. T. Harrington, then president of Texas A&M. His message was terse and not that friendly. To paraphrase it, "Be in my office Wednesday morning at 0800." That meant we were thus destined to miss day three of our finals. But at that point in time, maybe the end was near? In so many ways. I was no longer sure of the year, let alone the day. I found myself wondering if I would have to surrender my Aggie ring.

The next morning, right after chow, cadets Hagler and Rollins stood tall in Dr. Harrington's office promptly at 0800. We had not a single clue as to what was about to transpire.

An emergency meeting of the Board of Regents had been hurriedly called, and as my aged memory crawls backward more than half a century, I can recall Dr. Harrington ushering the two of us into an adjacent room where he ominously commanded us, "Have a seat, gentlemen. I will visit with you both later."

While Jon quietly contemplated the total wreckage that was probably going to befall his outstanding record of accomplishment and his unfettered eight-lane career path, my thoughts tended to be more basic. Would I be shot or hanged? Also, would my Bull Ring credits be erased? Basic stuff.

The suspense continued to mount when the Board of Regents adjourned at midday for lunch, and when the assembled horde of media types pressed for a situational update, Dr. Harrington brushed them aside by telling them there were no announcements to be made.

Our feelings of utter doom and depression deepened. Along about 2:00 p.m., the door opened and a smiling Dr. Harrington announced, "Coach Jim Myers has accepted our offer to become athletic director and head football coach for Texas A&M."

The deal was done. Another Kodak moment. I think my heart actually stopped beating.

The assembled throng, who by then knew of our trip to Iowa, pushed Hagler and me in the direction of Dr. Harrington, who draped his arm around each of our trembling shoulders. When asked if we would be given the opportunity to take our exams, he did the politically correct thing—even though there was no such thing as "politically correct" at that time—and indicated that permission to take our exams would be at the discretion of our professors. He also, through gritted teeth, I sensed, gave the two of us a less-than-enthusiastic pat on the back for the job we had done.

Let's get real here, folks! I was a B student for the most part. Jon was an A student. My fears ran deeper than Jon's. I had an ace in the hole, so to speak. I had strongly supported the Faculty Athletic Selection Committee and its role, so I was ultimately allowed to take the finals I had missed. The record will show I was very handsomely rewarded for my actions on behalf of the faculty.

Jon, of course, made straight A's. But he would have made A's anytime and every time he took the exams. If anyone from Texas A&M ever exemplified a straight-A life and career, it would be Jon Hagler.

It was a wild, crazy time and—up to that moment—was either one of the bravest things each of us ever did or the stupidest.

The next week, *Sports Illustrated* ran a short item about the Iowa State Athletic Department's picking up the tab for the Hagler-Rollins Head Coach Raid wintertime field trip. I never received a bill. A generous Aggie in Houston whose name is familiar to everyone at Texas A&M University

Press paid for our airplane tickets. The *Fort Dodge Messenger* described it as "the best panty raid ever."

Jim Myers's career at Texas A&M was shorter and less successful than all would have hoped. But he graced the Dallas Cowboys coaching staff as an assistant head coach for many years. He passed away in retirement a few years ago but is fondly remembered as a Christian man who bled maroon until the very end. In 2007, in an impressive ceremony, he presented that tattered, yellowed, eighty-foot telegram that helped convince him Texas A&M was the place where any head football coach would want to coach. Once upon a time, that relic telegram was displayed in the Lettermen's Lounge. Where is it today? I haven't a clue.

Truly, that was the week that was for yours truly.

Chapter 35

Smokey Harper

The Rest of the Story

What was it like to be a college athletic trainer in 1927 in the South? Athletic trainers—at institutions that had trainers—were on their own. The profession had only been in existence forty-five years; there was no such job before that time. They were starting very close to ground zero. There was no place one could go to learn the ins and outs of athletic training, except to be one. As in Smokey's case, almost to a man, athletic trainers were former athletes. It was basically self-taught and on-the-job training. With the exception of over-the-counter medications, ointments, and liniment, all they had to work with were their hands—massage (rubdowns) and bandages. For serious injuries and health problems, referral to a physician was their only option.

It should also be remembered that the medical profession, by the turn of the twentieth century, was just slightly ahead of the athletic training field, but medicine would progress faster than athletic training. The medical licensing pressures of the latter half of the 1800s had, by that time, finally required that physicians be certified and meet some kind of universally accepted knowledge requirement. They were now licensed in all the states. Education for doctors had taken a giant step forward in the last decade of the 1800s, when Johns Hopkins University began requiring a candidate wishing to enter medical school to have first earned a four-year degree. Once a student was admitted, the curriculum would include two years of lab sciences plus two years of clinicals. Other medical schools began to follow this concept.

A college curriculum for athletic trainers, however, was decades in the future, with licensing and certification requirements to follow. Progress was, however, inching forward ever so slowly.

A substitute for rubber-based adhesives, which were also an irritant, emerged when the first zinc-based tape for athletic taping was made available by Johnson & Johnson in 1899. Dr. Bilik first published *Athletic Training* in 1917, a comprehensive book on appropriate athletic training and medical techniques. Subsequent editions, later titled *The Trainer's Bible,* were updated as new procedures and approaches were introduced. In 1918 the Cramer brothers started the Cramer Chemical Company and produced items specifically for use by athletic trainers. Their first product was athletic liniment. Those resources were by no means the only materials and publications available to athletic trainers during the early 1900s, but those developments were few and far between and are indicative of the state of materials available to trainers when Smokey began.

Matt J. Weber states in *Dropping the Bucket and Sponge: A History of Early Athletic Training, 1881–1947* that the Carnegie Foundation for the Advancement of Teaching released a report on existing practices in intercollegiate athletics in 1929. The study and report were driven by vocal concerns from college faculties regarding problems they had identified resulting from the growth of intramural athletic programs, particularly football. As expected, the report's findings were biased toward higher education faculties, which had provided impetus for the study.

Samuel Bilik, MD, who authored and published the aforementioned *Trainers Bible*, had this to say in response to the Carnegie report:

> At most of the colleges visited, the position of trainer lacks definition. At some, the value of his work is questionable. As regards football, it is rare indeed that his functions include the conditioning of the team or squad, the coach confining his own efforts to the specialized technical instruction of his players.
>
> The result is that, sometime gradually, sometimes abruptly, the trainer's duties have developed into supervising the equipment and its care, rendering first aid when the team physician is not available, and under the team physician's direction, applying massage, baking, and other forms of physiotherapy. Although, among trainers an experience of twenty years is not uncommon, yet in few instances has this experience been preceded by any scientific training. As a not infrequent result, tradition, superstition, and prejudice have usurped

> the place that should be filled by scientific reason and knowledge; the trainer's locker has become a quack cabinet overflowing with proprietary ointments, liniments, and washes, and his quarters a museum of old and new appliances for applying heat, water, light, massage, and electricity. The trainer who, having acquired a foundation of anatomical knowledge, realizes the functions of his calling and knows its boundaries with reference to the work of the team physician, is rare indeed. (Weber, *Dropping the Bucket and Sponge*, 338–39)

This was the landscape for treatment of athletic injuries and looking after the health of college athletes in 1926, when the rookie Clemson athletic trainer, Smokey Harper, embarked on his first football season. Where did he fit in professionally; where did he go from this beginning point?

A thread that is woven into his entire career is obvious. Smokey was loyal to the head coaches for whom he had worked, and he understood his role as trainer within each of the head coach's support staff's organization. At first glance, those characteristics are plain and simple behaviors, but inside the cauldron of something as enormously competitive as college athletics, and especially football, they are the difference between positive and negative results. In addition to the technical constructs of the athletic trainer's duties, he also has a role to play within the day-to-day organization as set in motion by the head coach and reflecting his own personality. This is sometime called being the "right fit."

Another takeaway from Smokey's career is the value those head coaches for whom he worked placed on their need for Smokey to be a part of their staff. As pointed out previously, the head coaches for whom he worked were at the top of their profession. They knew what it took to be successful, and he fit into their schemes for achieving their goals.

Within the athletic training profession, Harper was unique. He was a participant within professional organizations but did not seek leadership positions. College degrees were a requirement for many of those positions, and Smokey was a collegiate dropout, so he never pushed that envelope. But much more importantly, that is not where he fit into the athletic training craft.

Smokey Harper was a teacher. He was a practitioner of the learning construct that one acquires by hands-on doing: practice. He would teach a neophyte student trainer how to perform a particular technique—say, tape an ankle—and then that student trainer was put to work taping ankles. The teacher unobtrusively observed from a distance. One step farther: when the more experienced student trainer had mastered a technique or procedure, he allowed that student to train the neophyte. Both learned from that experience.

His approach to developing student trainers created a bond of trust, enhanced their self-esteem, and encouraged reaching out toward new boundaries. He never raised his voice, condemned, or lost patience when problems arose. Those characteristics alone made Smokey unique.

When players who, Smokey knew, were concerns of the coaching staff would come into the training room, he had a way of admonishing them that helped get the coaching staff's point across in a nonthreatening way. Conversely, players could pull pranks at his expense, and he would laugh with them. It was all in fun and he joined them.

The relationship with the head coaches for whom he worked has already been addressed from the view of his fitting into the coach-trainer-player dynamic. But what about Smokey's athletic training skills? By the time he arrived at Texas A&M and after twenty-eight years in the profession, Smokey had probably forgotten more about athletic training than many of his colleagues knew. Along the way, had he been considered an incompetent or even an *average* athletic trainer, those highly driven and motivated bosses would not have kept him on their payrolls.

The athletic training profession was changing rapidly in the 1950s. Yet it is appropriate to revisit two points in the previous Bilik quote:

1. In 1954 the athletic trainer at Texas A&M was in charge of ordering and maintaining equipment;
2. The trainer was not involved with conditioning; this was handled by the coaching staff.

Athletic training was still a few years away from being innately tied to medicine, as it is today. This modern relationship is borne out by the medical emphasis and physician association as stated in the National Athletic Trainers Association's (NATA) statement describing the modern athletic trainer: "Athletic trainers are health care professionals who collaborate with physicians."

Smokey supervised between five and seven student trainers; he was the only full-time, professional athletic trainer on Texas A&M's campus. Either he or a student trainer covered basketball and baseball games and track and field meets, *if requested*. Coaches of the separate sports or their student managers handled their day-to-day minor training requirements. Need for treatment or injury during practices necessitated coming to the training room underneath the stadium at Kyle Field. Training room appliances were whirlpool, hydro collator (hot, wet pads), diathermy, and ultrasound. The team physician was a local general practitioner, Henry Harrison, MD; the team's orthopedic physician was located in Houston. The campus hospital provided necessary overnight stays requiring nursing care.

Fast-forward to today. The head athletic trainer is flanked by any number of other assistant trainer professionals; the number an institution should have on staff is determined by a NATA-devised formula. All have earned their degrees from an accepted athletic training curriculum or a medically related degree program. They are licensed—most states require it—and they are certified by the NATA Board of Certification. Student trainers today touch players only under direct supervision of certified professional trainers.

Today there are better diagnostic tools for referral, including MRI and CT scans, blood studies, cardiac monitors for conditioning, and nerve conduction studies. There are better protective rules before a player returns to action after injury (i.e., the concussion protocol). We have better rehabilitation tools, including stress EKG, underwater exercise pools, and video capabilities to show athletes what they are doing right and wrong. New physical therapy modalities are available. Uniforms are improved with better protection. Nutrition and off-season conditioning have improved, based on scientific study. And of course there are many new surgical procedures, including arthroscopy, a less invasive surgical technique that leads to better stabilization and quicker healing. Today's trainers utilize more bracing and less casting, permitting an earlier return to better range of motion.

So much has changed. And yet Charles Edwin Harper—known as Smokey for most of his life—was a pioneer in the field of athletic training. Like pioneers from other times and walks of life, he took what he had to work with and made the best of it. Smokey took others from later generations and molded them into future athletic trainers, assisting and encouraging them along the way by leading them from behind. Beyond being a competent technician, he was also an astute judge of those young athletes he treated and cared for, not just of their athletic talent and physical being but also their inner self. It was that insight, when combined with his easy fit in the organization, that made him so valuable to head coaches who were at the top of their profession.

Smokey was in the fourth quarter of his career when we worked under his direction during the Bryant era at Texas A&M. His treatment methods and the modalities he used were, for the most part, not those in use today. Likewise, are not the lifestyles of the 1920s, 1930s, 1940s, and 1950s considered archaic by those who did not live through those times?

Athletic training and the camaraderie it provided with coaches and young athletes was literally his life, after his family. That fact was no better exemplified than by his answer to a question on a personal profile sheet he completed for the University of Alabama's Sports Publicity Office: "Hobbies: None."

For that kind of devotion to his life's work, this obscure athletic trainer—Smokey Harper—was inducted into the Southeast Athletic Trainers' Association Hall of Fame, the Southwest Athletic Trainers' Association Hall of Fame, and the National Athletic Trainers Association Hall of Fame.

Afterword

When Billy Pete Was Just a Lad

As this book was entering production at Texas A&M University Press, the Aggie Nation learned of the passing of Billy Pete Huddleston on Wednesday, July 31, 2019. His unmatchable life and career ended at his Double H Ranch near Navasota. There are countless stories about this fine Texas Aggie, and there were numerous teammates, classmates, Aggies from all over the world, and family members who wanted to share their own personal recollections about one of the most famous, totally deserving Texas Aggies who ever wore a Texas A&M senior ring.

Billy Pete Huddleston was, without question, the most successful of not just the Junction Boys but of all the Texas Aggies who played football during the Bryant era. He left both a gigantic footprint and a gaping hole in every teammate's heart. And, in the end, Billy Pete Huddleston probably epitomized the very best end result that Coach Paul Bryant wanted from each and every Texas Aggie footballer.

Here's a direct quote from Dave Campbell's recently released *Favorite Texas College Football Stories*, a Texas A&M University Press book. Huddleston said, "At my senior year's Texas A&M football banquet, Coach Bryant asked me to stand, and he said these words: 'I want my son to grow up like this young man.'" Paul Bryant Jr., now trustee emeritus of the Board of Trustees at the University of Alabama, would undoubtedly endorse that sage observation.

When the Texas Aggies teed it up against the vaunted Rice Owls in November 1954 in Houston at Rice Stadium, Billy Pete, the Aggie left halfback, was listed in the game day program at five feet eleven and 165 pounds. He later gained about ten pounds, but some say he topped out at five feet nine, maximum. However, one of his teammates said this about Billy Pete:

"He wasn't that big and not really that fast, but he was like trying to catch a cottontail rabbit. He'd zig and zag and then he'd turn into a jackrabbit."

Let's start with a brief Texas history lesson. Before we delve into Billy Pete Huddleston's pre-A&M life, you need to know something about his hometown. The tiny town of Iraan is in Pecos County—think Permian Basin and West Texas—and we can trace the initial development of the community back to the late 1920s.

Ira G. Yates and his wife, Anna, generously donated 152 acres of their 20,000-acre Yates Ranch for the townsite. According to Gerald McLeod, an *Eagle* columnist, the daughter of a ranch hand suggested the name of the town to be a blend of Ira and Anna. Her entry won the contest, and she pocketed the princely sum of $1,000 as her prize for naming the town.

Locals call their town by one of two "accepted" pronunciations. One is just like the Middle Eastern country. The other is "all one word" with but a breath of a break between the two combined words.

By the end of the 1920s, the Yates Ranch was struggling, mainly from an extended drought. But Yates was motivated to approach a San Angelo–based oil outfit to explore for oil on his property.

A great decision, that's for sure! On just the fourth test well, a gusher erupted that covered a tent city four miles away. On Yates's sixty-seventh birthday, he was handed an $18 million oil royalty check. (Try to resist converting that sum to current dollars.)

One local wag said, "Folks had to be careful when they were digging holes for their tomatoes. Dig too deep, and you'll probably hit oil!

After a number of corporate maneuvers, the Yates Ranch ultimately became the birthplace of Marathon Oil. And Billy Pete worked for them for a few years as a petroleum engineer.

Enough history. Back to Billy Pete. He would probably tell you his side of the story because he was a superb storyteller. As the Aggie friends, employees, teammates, and classmates seized upon the opportunity to share their favorite stories about Billy Pete, it occurred to me that were he still with us, he would undoubtedly enjoy hearing those stories as they were shared among friends and family.

Hundreds of Texas A&M petroleum engineers around the globe enjoyed a personal relationship with Billy Pete Huddleston. Here's how that happened.

For seventeen years, at absolutely no cost to Texas A&M, Billy Pete Huddleston would conduct two classes weekly. In the fall semester, the class began at noon and ran until 3:00 p.m. The fall course was mandatory for senior petroleum engineering majors. But the spring course was elective. Still, everyone attended. Basically, one of the courses was economic, and the other was on business practices.

Jay Graham, a member of the Class of '92 and, among other things, a member of the Texas A&M Board of Regents, recalled the days when he sat in a classroom and was mesmerized by the lectures offered up by one of the oil and gas industry's giants—Billy Pete Huddleston. Those young senior Aggie PetE majors looked upon Huddleston as the real deal; he talked the talk and walked the walk. His classroom sermons preached the rules of fair play, honesty, reliability, concern for your fellow man—with an emphasis on fellow Texas Aggies—and hard work. It became apparent that he regarded his employees as extensions of his own family.

And for that reason, as years passed, many of the top PetE majors reached out to Billy Pete Huddleston. Some were hired. Many were given a hand up in some way or another. One feature stuck out: "If you want to be successful, hang out with successful people."

Graham recounted that there came a time in his career when he was in his mid-thirties and stuck on the middle rungs of the ladder to success. He called Billy Pete and told him he was planning to strike out and open his own company.

"I explained my situation" Graham said, "and was surprised when he asked, 'What took you so long?'"

From that point forward, things moved almost too rapidly. Billy Pete said, "I want to help you because I believe in you. I am going to stake you to $5,000,000. But you will definitely need more that that kind of funding." In short order, one of his prospects was contacted by phone, and a meeting was arranged with a contact from Dallas.

Graham had no office, no phone, no business cards. He did have a rock-solid commitment of support for his new venture. Sidestepping the fact that Graham had no office, Billy Pete suggested that Graham invite his prospect to the Houston office of Huddleston & Company.

The morning of the meeting, Graham entered the main conference room, where he found Billy Pete waiting for the arrival of the prospective investor. When the fellow arrived, Billy Pete said, "This young man was one of my finest petroleum engineering students at Texas A&M. He is a talented fellow and I believe in him. I am going to back him to the tune of $5,000,000, and I think he would be a good investment for you, too."

Then he left.

Simply stated, the prospect matched the funding suggested and also departed. Thus, Graham's first day of his new company—with no office and no phone or business cards—concluded on a bright note, with $10 million in the bank.

The record will show that Graham performed exceptionally well and delivered a handsome return on that initial investment. Today Jay Graham remains one of Billy Pete's most successful petroleum engineers to come out of Texas A&M.

Graham, by the way, is deeply involved in the Texas A&M Lettermen's Association and holds his high school record for single-game strikeouts. It's a great story, but you'll have to ask him yourself. Today's main topic is Billy Pete Huddleston.

One of Billy Pete's teammates was the starting center, Herb Wolf, a movie-star-handsome fellow who hailed from Stephen F. Austin High School in Houston. Wolf was an architecture major, and although he enjoyed a goodly number of productive years as an architect, his one true love was painting. And he was good at his craft, both with oils and watercolors.

Herb and his wife worked as a team, and there came a time when he wanted to stage his very first art show in Houston. They rented a venue and carefully staged the displays of his artwork, anticipating opening the doors the following day at 8:30 a.m.

Wolf and his wife, Sue, arrived about 8:15 a.m. and were greeted by an attendant who gleefully reported that "some man" had showed up at 8:00 and purchased twenty-four of the forty-eight pieces of artwork. He left behind a check that was . . . well, let's simply say it was a generous offering. Billy Pete strikes again!

Bennie Sinclair was an All-SWC end on the Aggies football team and a PetE major as well. Sinclair and Billy Pete bonded shortly after graduation, and together they accomplished some very remarkable things. Sinclair confessed that, thanks to Billy Pete, he won't be standing in any "bread lines" anytime this century.

Billy Pete Huddleston was truly a one-of-a-kind Texas Aggie. He cared far more about giving than he did receiving, and he avoided the spotlight as he forged an absolutely remarkable career in the oil and gas industry.

His wife, Flossie, was his original business partner, but he did a superb job preparing his offspring to carry on the family's business precisely as he had done when he was holding the wheel.

They simply don't make them like Billy Pete Huddleston anymore. But there are, quite literally, thousands of Texas A&M–reared petroleum engineers from Texas that now form the backbone of the global petroleum engineering profession. They forged their respective careers using Billy Pete's style of business as their model. It works—every time.

From that tiny town in the dead-center of the Permian Basin to the enormous campus at Texas A&M University, the gigantic shadow of Billy Pete Huddleston serves as both an example and a reminder that Aggies never quit. He leaves behind hundreds of thousands of Aggies who admire everything he ever did and seek to emulate that special spirit of Aggieland that will live forever.

Index